# BRACE READING

# READING

## PLAIN & SIMPLE

# FACE
# READING

## PLAIN & SIMPLE

JONATHAN DEE

THE ONLY BOOK YOU'LL EVER NEED

HAMPTON ROADS

Illustrations © 2018 Hampton Roads Publishing Company, Inc.

Cover design by Jim Warner
Interior design by Kathryn Sky-Peck

Hampton Roads Publishing Company, Inc.
Charlottesville, VA 22906
Distributed by Red Wheel/Weiser, LLC
www.redwheelweiser.com

Sign up for our newsletter and special offers by going to
www.redwheelweiser.com/newsletter/

ISBN: 978-1-57174-784-6

Library of Congress Cataloging-in-Publication Data
Names: Dee, Jonathan, 1957-2010, author.
Title: Face reading plain & simple / Jonathan Dee.
Other titles: Face reading plain and simple
Description: Charlottesville : Hampton Roads Pub., 2018.
Identifiers: LCCN 2018003345 | ISBN 9781571747846 (5.5 x 8 pbk. : alk. paper)
Subjects: LCSH: Physiognomy.
Classification: LCC BF851 .D385 2018 | DDC 138--dc23
LC record available at https://lccn.loc.gov/2018003345

Printed in the United States of America

IBI

10 9 8 7 6 5 4 3 2 1

# Contents

# Introduction

The Chinese art of face reading, or *kang xiang* as it was originally known, has a very long history indeed. The ancient sages who formulated this practice are long forgotten, having lived more than two thousand years ago. Even so, they drew on the core beliefs of oriental philosophy to provide the basis for this fascinating study. Even though face reading originated in China, it does not apply only to oriental features. In fact, ethnic type is not important, because face reading's rules and interpretations can be applied to all racial groups equally.

In face reading, like Chinese astrology, feng shui, and oriental medicine, we find Chinese concepts that have become familiar, such as yang and yin and the five elements of wood, fire, earth, metal, and water. In fact, face reading has a great deal in common with feng shui, because in this art, the human face is regarded as a landscape with five "mountains"—the brow, the nose, the two cheekbones, and the chin—each symbolically associated with one of the five elements. This facial landscape also possesses four "rivers"—the eyes, the nostrils, the ears, and the mouth. Each feature is a component in this landscape and each is interpreted accordingly.

One can find each year of life marked on the face. The traditions of Chinese face reading state that no less than ninety-two age positions are dotted around the face. Apart from these, there are also twelve "Palaces of Fortune," which give information about specific issues such as partnerships, career, wealth, and health.

Even without this knowledge, we all routinely assess the personality of others by their faces. However, it is not usually the physical features of the face that we assess, but the transitory nature of the expressions. In Chinese face reading, it is the actual formation of the features, their balance, and their symmetry that are the important factors, as well as the overall shape of the face.

There are five basic face shapes, each associated with one of the five elements. As well as these, there are two variations known, respectively, by comparisons with a bucket and a volcano.

The shape of individual features has the greatest complexity. There are twenty-three basic shapes of eyes, twenty-three conformations of eyebrows, thirteen types of ears, thirteen basic nose profiles, and nine types of mouths. I describe each one in the pages of this book, as well as other features, such as the cheekbones, the width and height of the brow, the cheek lines, or *fa ling*, and the philtrum, or *jen chung*.

It is somewhat unfortunate that the ancient Chinese sages who formulated face reading were extremely sexist. However, although most of the traditions of this ancient art are concerned with the interpretation of masculine features, they can be applied to female faces too. While we are on the subject, throughout the book the pronouns "he" and "his" have been used. I assure you that this is not an indication of the author's sexist attitudes; it is simply a method to avoid the awkwardness of writing "he or she" or "his or her" repeatedly.

Every face has its own story to tell, and the art of kang xiang will show you how to read every feature, line, and wrinkle and discover aspects of the personalities of your family and friends that you never knew existed. After all, Chinese face reading literally demonstrates that one's features are an open book!

# The Divisions of the Face

1

The ancient Chinese sages divided the face into a bewildering number of sections. There are no fewer than 130 individual physical features that can be interpreted. It's a good thing that we don't have to concern ourselves with each one of them; for a beginner, it is more than enough to start with the three basic regions dividing the face into horizontal sections.

## The Three Primary Divisions of the Face

### The Celestial Region or Upper Zone

The celestial or heavenly facial division occupies the area of the brow. It extends across the upper part of the face between the hairline and the eyebrows. A wide, well-proportioned forehead is considered to be generally fortunate. However, for a brow that is too wide—giving the whole face the impression of being a downward-pointed triangle—the outlook is not that good for the love life. If the brow is smooth, even, clear, and free of blemishes, it suggests a happy childhood, a fulfilling home life, and a supportive, loving family. On the other hand, the opposite is the case if the celestial region appears to be lumpy or scarred or possesses a dull, grayish skin tone.

The celestial region is further subdivided into three horizontal areas (see page 4). The area closest to the hairline relates to imagination, the brow region is associated with memory, and the area located just above the eyebrows is concerned with observation (see chapter 3, The Brow, on page 37).

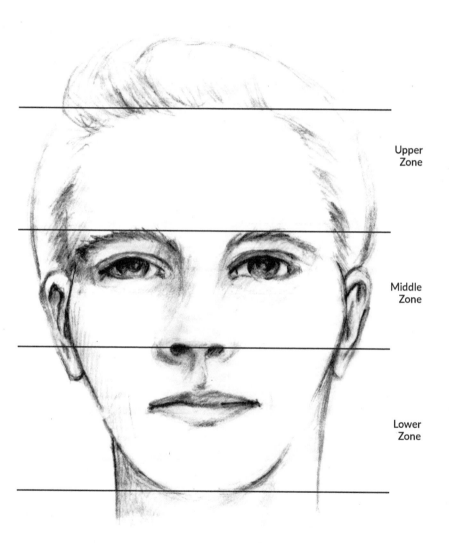

Upper
Zone

Middle
Zone

Lower
Zone

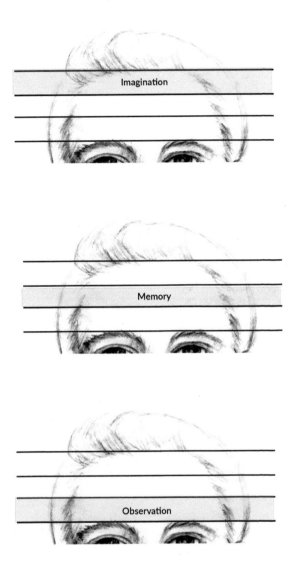

The three subdivisions of the Upper Zone

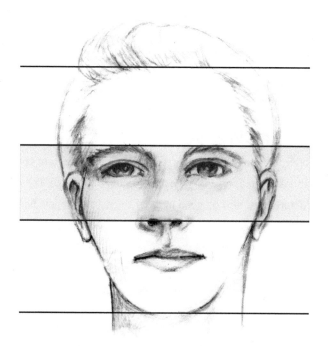

## The Region of Self-Will or Middle Zone

The region of self-will is otherwise referred to as the "human region" or the "region of humanity." It extends across the central portion of the face and is home to the eyes, nose, cheekbones, and ears. Ideally, each of these features should be well proportioned in relation to each of the others. The more regular the features in this area, the more settled the individual. Any feature that is disproportionately large will have an unfortunate effect, especially in affairs of the heart.

If this region is longer than the other two, then willpower and leadership potential are indicated. There is an ability to seize control of complex situations and turn them to personal advantage.

If the skin tone in the region of self-will is clear and smooth, this indicates financial good fortune in youth and middle age. If it is blotchy or scarred, or if the skin tone has a grayish tinge, then the outlook for material life is not so promising.

## The Earthly Region or Lower Zone

Proportion and a good balance of features are important considerations when assessing the earthly region of the face. The bone structure must also be good in order to ensure a happy, healthy, and prosperous old age. The lips and mouth, as well as the configuration of the chin, are the most revealing factors here. Full lips combined with a strong chin are signs of a strong constitution, while thin lips and a receding chin denote frail health.

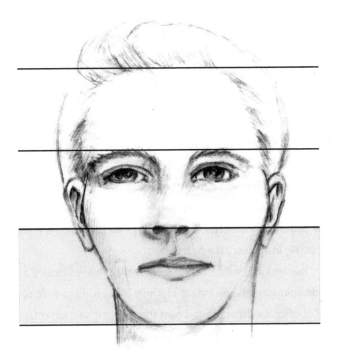

A perfectly formed face

An imperfectly formed face

## The Secondary Divisions of the Face

### The Five Predominant Features

The five predominant features of the face are, predictably enough, the eyes, the eyebrows, the mouth, the nose, and the ears. If these features are regular and in proportion both to each other and to the general shape of the face, then this is a good indication of prosperity, health, and good fortune. However, should one or more of these features give a visual impression of being "out of line" or "misplaced," then fortunes will suffer. An inwardly turned eye, a bent, crooked, or broken nose, a scarred eyebrow, and a twisted lip are all features that detract from a harmonious life. This said, it may be that despite one (or more) features that fall far short of perfection, the others may be beautifully formed and provide a respite from a harsh fate.

### The Five Animal Mountains and the Four Rivers

The five predominant features also have a relation to the "five mountains." The ancient Chinese regarded the face as a landscape with physical features that can be compared with the features on a map. It is not surprising that the terminology of the equally ancient traditional practice of feng shui is also used to describe areas of the face, bearing in mind the geographical connotations of feng shui.

In feng shui, each direction, East, South, West, North, and Center, is symbolized by both an element and a symbolic figure.

- East relates to the wood element, and its image is a green dragon.

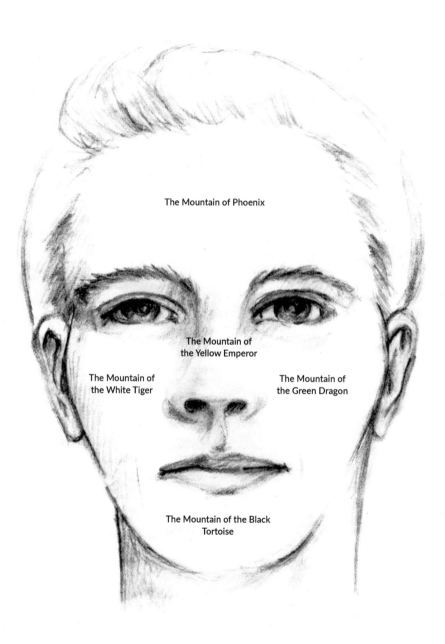

The Mountain of Phoenix

The Mountain of
the Yellow Emperor

The Mountain of
the White Tiger

The Mountain of
the Green Dragon

The Mountain of the Black
Tortoise

- South concerns the fire element and is symbolized by the phoenix or a red bird.

- West is connected to the metal element and is represented by the white tiger.

- North is the water direction, and its image is a black tortoise.

- The central space of anything or anyplace is symbolically connected to the Earth. Its color is yellow.

Likewise, in face reading, each prominent bony feature or ridge shares this symbolism, so the brow is considered the Mountain of the Phoenix; its element, fire, is emblematic of thought.

The left cheekbone is the Mountain of the Green Dragon, symbolizing the wood element.

The right cheekbone is the Mountain of the White Tiger, symbolic of the metal element.

The chin is considered watery and is called the Mountain of the Black Tortoise.

The nose, the central feature of the face, is referred to either as the Central Mountain or the Mountain of the Yellow Emperor.

Although they are not strictly part of Chinese face reading, in addition to the five mountains, the face also possesses the four rivers:

- the River Kong—the ears
- the River Ho—the eyes
- the River Wai—the mouth
- the River Chai—the nostrils

The four rivers are relevant in Chinese diagnostic practices, and these ideas are connected with the life force or *chi* energy. Chi, the universal breath of life, has two forms, positive and negative, *sheng chi* and *sha chi*, so each of the rivers has both positive and negative aspects. Chi arrives in the eyes in the form of light and is expelled as tears. Sound reaches the ears and is expelled as wax. Breath is the positive chi of the nostrils, while mucus is the negative chi, so only the mouth can both take in and expel chi as kind words or harsh ones, good food or bad.

## The Age Positions of the Face

The ancient traditions of face reading provide specific age positions, which are dotted about the face, ears, and crown. These positions serve to highlight particular years in a person's lifetime from zero to ninety. The most important of these are known as the thirteen significant positions. These thirteen positions are found in a straight vertical line running down the middle of the face from the hairline to the tip of the chin. Each of the thirteen points has an individual traditional name and refers to the most important years of life, ranging from fifteen to seventy-one.

### The Thirteen Significant Positions

#### 1 T'ien Chung—Age 15

This position literally means "Middle Heaven." It is found just below the midpoint of the hairline, and it relates to the fifteenth year of life. A scar, blemish, bump, or dent here denotes an unhappy childhood and a confused adolescence. A dark mark indicates early poverty. A vein running into the hairline at this point reveals an immature and accident-prone nature.

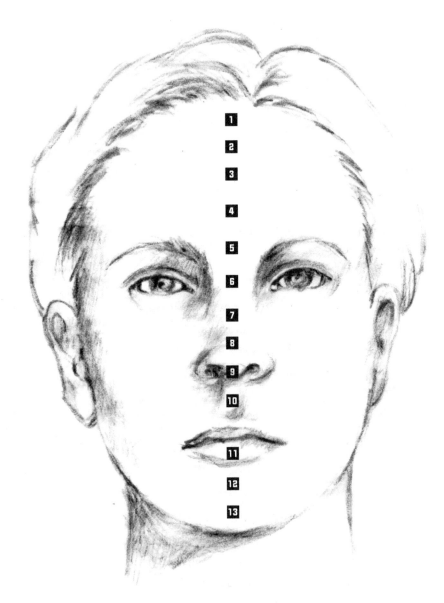

The thirteen significant positions

## 2 Tien T'ing—Age 18

This is the "Central Heaven" point, relating to early adulthood. If this area is unmarked and the complexion is clear, there is a good parental bond and the person can make loyal and influential friends. If any blemish permanently marks this area, the individual will find it hard to win goodwill. It is considered a bad omen if such a mark appears spontaneously. This kind of blemish is called a "Black Cloud," and it foretells a grave misfortune that will occur very soon.

## 3 Ssu K'ung—Age 21

If this area has no markings at all, then the fortunes in the twenty-first year are neutral. However, a red or yellow mark or tinge to the skin is considered to be a very good omen, denoting good advice and the liking and respect of others. A gray or black mark here indicates a bumpier path through life, with periods of bad luck, especially related to the career.

## 4 Chung Cheng—Age 24

If there is no blemish and the skin tone is good, then early successes are forecast. If this area is dented or discolored, the subject may lack concentration and application. A black mole here is the worst omen, indicating a severe lack of patience and the unfortunate tendency to be in the wrong place at the wrong time.

## 5 Yin T'ang—Age 27

This is a very important age point, and it connects closely to the interpretation of the eye brows (see chapter 5, The Eyebrows, on page 75). Good, clear skin here predicts a large inheritance and/

or shrewd business sense. A black mole here is said to signify a long illness, while a mole or any color to one side of this point can indicate legal problems. A scar or birthmark on the yin t'ang is traditionally said to reveal adoption. Eyebrows that meet can show that this person cannot be trusted to act honorably or truthfully. Eyebrows that nearly meet—the gap between them being very small—can denote complex legal issues that will occupy much of the twenty-seventh year.

### 6  Shan Ken—Age 40

This is the transition point between the celestial region and the region of self-will. This area should possess a noticeable but gentle dip to ensure a harmonious flow of energies between the two regions. If a dark patch of skin is found, it can indicate periods of recurring illness. In fact, illness of short duration is often foretold by the appearance of such a dark patch. As usual in face reading, the darker the area, the longer the ailment will last. A mole directly on the shan ken reveals a move away from home to find work. However, if the mole is off-center, then digestive problems are likely.

### 7  Nien Shang—Age 43

This area is located at the lower end of the nasal bone, and it concerns both health and the emotional life. A mole found here is indicative of a turbulent romantic life, as well as revealing recurring stomach upsets in the forty-third year.

### 8  Shou Shang—Age 44

This point is found midway between the end of the nasal bone and the tip of the nose. Clear, unblemished skin in this area reveals excellent fashion sense and a strong constitution. However, a prominent lump in this area suggests failed business enterprises. The presence of a mole is bad news for romantic prospects this year.

### 9  Chun T'ou—Age 47

The chun t'ou is found at the very tip of the nose, and it relates to finances in the forty-seventh year. A clear complexion is obviously a good omen for prosperity. A permanent red spot or mole on the chun t'ou is also considered beneficial to finances; however, noticeably open pores or dark hairs growing here are indicative of poverty.

### 10  Jen chung—Age 50

This area corresponds to the philtrum, the hollow between the nose and the lips. It relates to the fiftieth year of life, and it is considered so important that a whole chapter of this book is devoted to its interpretation.

### 11  Shui Hsing—Age 59

The shui hsing is located on the lower lip and is interpreted along with the mouth and tongue.

### 12  Ch'eng Chiang—Age 69

This area is found on the upper chin. It is considered a "watery" area of the face. It therefore is connected to both travel by water and drinking liquids. Should a dark patch appear here, it is advised that voyages be postponed and drinking limited until the patch fades. Pale, dark red, or greenish patches traditionally indicate poisoning or at the very least an infection acquired by drinking impure liquids.

### 13  Ti Ko—Age 70

The ti ko is the tip of the chin.

# The Twelve Palaces of the Face

As well as the multitude of age points on the face, there are also areas called the twelve Palaces of Fortune. These perform a function similar to that of the astrological houses in horoscopes. The palaces deal with specific topics such as relationships, material wealth, health, home, and so on. Some are found in only one location, such as the tip of the nose or the center of the brow, but others are divided between two areas, such as the regions below each eye or on each temple.

Assessing the twelve Palaces of Fortune provides a background to face reading as a whole and gives important clues as to how a person's life will progress.

### 1 Kaun Lu Kung—The Palace of Career

As well as representing the twenty-first year, this area is an important indicator of career and business success throughout life. In addition, an unblemished, perfectly formed central brow area shows the help of influential people. However, if this area is sunken, or too prominent, it suggests that there will be great obstacles to overcome. A mole here shows the need for diligence and perseverance.

### 2 Chine I Kung—The Palace of Movement

There are two Palaces of Movement, and each corresponds to one of the temples. These areas should be sunken, with no prominent bones or lumps. If this is the case, the person can expect successful journeys throughout life. A particularly fine complexion in these areas shows an adventurous personality. Any sudden

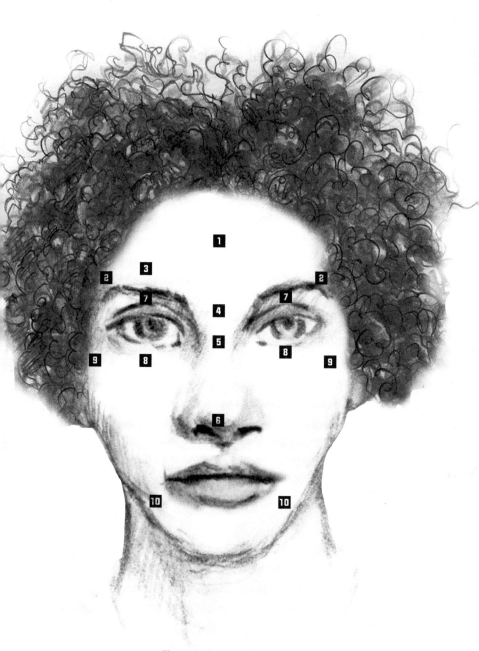

The twelve Palaces of Fortune

appearance of dark patches in the Palace of Movement shows that any trips the person has planned should be delayed until the dark patches have cleared up. Moles on either temple suggest danger from theft or suffering an accident while traveling.

### 3  Hsiung Ti Kung—The Palace of Brothers

The two areas directly above the eyebrows form the Palace of Brothers. This palace refers not only to near blood kin, but also to any people to whom the subject becomes attached throughout life. Long, well-formed eyebrows show happy, contented relationships with siblings and close friends. Broken, patchy, or scarred eyebrows indicate troublesome relationships.

### 4  Min Kung—The Palace of Life

The Palace of Life is concerned with the general emotional state. It is found in the same area as the shan ken, that is, directly between the eyebrows. Wrinkles found here in youth indicate turbulent love affairs; however, an absence of wrinkles after the age of thirty reveals a time waster and daydreamer. As usual, a good complexion with no blemishes indicates a fortunate emotional life.

### 5  Chi O Kung—The Palace of Sickness

Although this palace's name is unpleasant, it simply refers to the person's general state of health. It is found in the same area as the nien shang, on the bridge of the nose. Healthy signs are a good complexion, absence of blemishes, and a good, defined nose shape. However, should this area be crisscrossed with small lines or disfigured by a scar or mole, then the state of the constitution is not good, and many minor illnesses are foretold.

## 6  Ts'ai Pai Kung—The Palace of Wealth

As the name implies, this palace is concerned with material issues. It is found at the tip of the nose in the same position as the chun t'ou, so it relates to the forty-seventh year. A dark blemish here reveals a person who is too ready to accept responsibility and feels as though the weight of the world rests upon his shoulders. A scar here is a bad sign for prosperity, while a red mark or a particularly mobile nose tip is considered fortunate for finances.

## 7  T'ien Chai Kung—The Palace of House and Farm

This palace is found in two areas, each between the upper eyelid and the eyebrow. It relates not only to domestic life and family matters, but also to pets and livestock. If these areas are clear, with a good complexion, all will be well, but if they are scarred or of a very dark color, the subject will be a worrier. A mole on either eyelid indicates that some portion of the subject's life will be afflicted by poverty.

## 8  Nan Nu Kung—The Palace of Man and Woman

This palace is also concerned with family affairs. It is found in two areas, directly below the eyes. Naturally, the type of eye and the condition of the surrounding tissue are very relevant to establishing the fortunes predicted by this palace. Many crossed lines here suggest leaving the family home at an early age. A distinct crisscross pattern denotes strained family relationships and lack of contact, which becomes more evident with the passing of the years. If this area is baggy, very gray, wrinkled, or lumpy, then the family will be a continuous source of worry to this person.

### 9 Ch'I Ch'ien Kung—The Palace of Wife and Mistress

The Palace of Wife and Mistress corresponds to the cheekbones and, as the name suggests, is concerned with the character of the "significant other" in a person's life. In men, the right cheek is most relevant to the assessment of this palace, and in the case of women, it is the left. If the skin here is very tight and shiny, marital relations will become strained. A dent here is a bad sign, indicating infidelity. A mole in this palace shows a flirtatious and possibly wicked nature. However, as long as the cheekbones are not too prominent and the skin of this area is clear of blemishes, then a good-natured, reliable, virtuous, and wise spouse is forecast.

### 10 Nu P'u Kung—The Palace of Servants

This palace describes the relationships and attitudes to subordinates and employees, as well as giving an indication about friendships and working relationships between equals. The Nu P'u Kung is found on either side of the chin. A good, well-rounded shape shows trusted friends who will defer to this person's wisdom. However, should this area be wrinkled or blemished or possess bad skin tone, scars, or pits, then the person will be tactless and make unnecessary enemies.

### 11 Fu Te Kung—The Palace of Fortune and Virtue

The Fu Te Kung is not strictly speaking a palace at all. It is taken to mean the transient facial expressions that reveal emotional states. Therefore, a frown indicating annoyance, tears revealing sadness, or a smile of happiness would be considered aspects of the palace of fortune and virtue. This is the only time when expressions are considered in Chinese face reading.

## 12 Hsiang Mao Kung—The Palace of the Countenance

Like the eleventh palace, this palace is not really an area of the face at all, but rather governs the overall impression one gives through one's physical features. In short, it is the art of Chinese face reading itself.

# The
## Shape
## of the Face

**2**

There are five basic face shapes, and these relate to the five Chinese elements of wood, fire, earth, metal, and water.

## The Five Agents of Transformation

The oriental sages of old believed that the universe was in a constant state of change. Over the centuries, the Chinese identified five stages of this cycle of constant states of transformation. To each they gave a name in the terms that were most familiar to them and accorded with their philosophy. Each of these stages is created by the one preceding it and, in turn, gives rise to the one that follows. The Chinese sages described these stages of existence as "agents of change" or "agents of transformation." In the West, we tend to call them "elements." In Chinese terms, these elements are wood, fire, earth, metal, and water. We have come across the elements in their guises as the five animal mountains of the face.

## The Creation Cycle

According to oriental symbolism, the elements can be arranged into a circular form known as "the Creation Cycle," a concept that will be familiar to anyone who takes an interest in feng shui or Chinese medicine. According to this cycle, wood is burned to feed fire, fire creates earth in the form of ash, and the depths of the earth give birth to metal, which, when molten, flows like water. Water in turn feeds the growth of wood. In short, each element does something to help the next element, thereby enhancing the entire cycle.

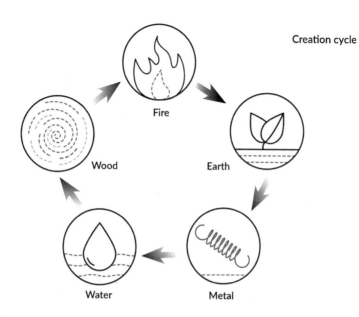

Creation cycle

Fire

Wood

Earth

Water

Metal

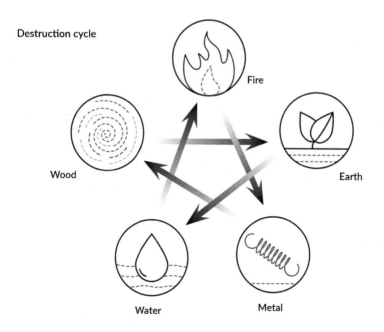

Destruction cycle

Fire

Wood

Earth

Water

Metal

However, should this progressive sequence be disrupted, chaos and destruction can occur. Beginning again with wood, wood exhausts earth, earth fouls water, water quenches fire, fire melts metal, and metal chops wood.

## The Cycle of Destruction

Apart from the obvious qualities of the elements, the traditions of China also endowed them with other attributes. These are particular compass directions, colors, symbolic animals, plants, sounds, smells, activities, and, most important to face reading, individual geometric shapes and their associated definitions of character. Thus, the element wood was symbolized by the rectangle, fire by the triangle, earth by the square, metal by the oval (or inverted triangle), and water by the circle. Thus, there are five basic face shapes, each of which has an association with one of the agents of change.

In addition to these five basic face shapes, there are also two variations that are recognized but do not strictly fit within the elemental system. These are "the volcano face," which is a variant of the fire type of face, and "the bucket face," which is of the metal type.

# Elemental Shapes

| Element | Shape |
| --- | --- |
| Wood | Rectangle |
| Fire | Triangle |
| Earth | Square |
| Metal | Oval or Inverted Triangle |
| Water | Circle |
| Volcano (fire variant) | Truncated Upward-Pointed Triangle |
| Bucket (metal variant) | Truncated Inverted Triangle |

## The Wood Face

The geometric shape associated with the wood element is the rectangle, so this type of face has a uniformity of width and is far longer than it is wide, giving it a rectangular appearance. The forehead of this type of face is high and is usually marked by well-defined creases. The general aspect of

this face is both genial and dignified. This is a face type associated with warmth and optimism. In men, this type of face is often accompanied by a receding hairline.

The possessor of the wood face is popular; he wins friends easily and has a charitable nature. He also demands that things are done his way, and although he means well, he can express himself in an arrogant manner because he can be tactless when imposing his views. This person is energetic, with leadership potential, strong ideals, and determination. He will stand up for a point of principle and he has a philosophical attitude toward life. Often, the possessor of the wood face is convinced of his own rightness in any situation, and since this face type is associated with strong religious or philosophical convictions, care must be taken that the sense of always being right does not turn a positive character trait into harmful fanaticism.

## The Fire Face

The shape symbolic of the fire element is the triangle. Likewise, the fiery type of face possesses a wide jaw and a narrow forehead. It therefore resembles an upward-pointing triangle. The

fire-faced person tends to be lucky, highly sexed, and physically attractive and can be extremely persuasive and charming. However, his boiling point is very low, and this subject can show an altogether less pleasant aspect when self-control is lost. Of course, extremes of this type can be physically explosive, and even the most relatively mild mannered fire-faced person usually has had a series of turbulent relationships in his life.

Those with a fire face are known for the angry look in their eyes. This can be quite daunting to all but the bravest souls. As might be imagined, the temperament of a person with a fire face is likely to be rather heated and excitable, possibly resulting from an unhappy childhood or a deprived background. This type is very ambitious, since there is a deep desire to remove himself as far from his origins as is humanly possible. This desire also provides a clue to the reasons for a lack of patience and outbursts of anger when plans go awry.

## The Earth Face

The geometric shape symbolic of the earth element means that this subject reflects the earth's own shape by having a height and width that are approximately the same. The complexion of the earth face tends to be ruddy, the hair often bushy, and the eyes somewhat red but expressive of author-ity. The nose and mouth also will tend to be wide, although the lips are often quite thin and the teeth small. A person with this type of face enjoys good health, has an active social life, and is probably very physical, to the point where he may become involved in contact sports at some point in his life.

The earth face is an indicator of tough-ness and determination, although some would claim that a more apt description involves total obstinacy. A person with an earth face has high energy levels and a tendency to leap to con-clusions before the facts are fully known. A person with an earth face often possesses a quick and unpredictable temper. This type of person is so impulsive that he can get himself into trouble with no help from anyone else. Those around him then become vital as his saviors because although he can get himself into trouble, he lacks the inner strength to extricate himself without consider-able help.

## The Metal Face

The metal face type is the opposite to that of fire. It is rather oval, but it is more easily visualized as an inverted triangle, wid-est at the top, with a pointed chin. The facial features are regular and rather refined; however, the mouth may be either slightly too

large or slightly too small. The large eyes are lively and active, denoting intelligence and sharp perceptions. In fact, a person with a metal face has a mind that is extremely active and rarely gives him any peace.

This person lives in his head, and he is inclined more toward an intel-lectual career than to manual work, but he might actually prefer it if it were not so. He has difficulty in relaxing and he may have been quite a difficult child. He loves to talk and he will not shy away from heated debate as long as he is sure of his ground. However, even when he is not, he is quite capable of overwhelming his opponent with a clever use of words and sharp wit. Although he likes meeting new people, he will keep all but a few at a distance because emotional closeness is disturbing to him. A person with a metal face is a born politician, salesperson, and organizer. He is likely to be ambitious and shrewd and can be quite cunning when the occasion demands it.

## The Water Face

The geometric shape of the water element is the circle, so the water face is easy to recognize simply because it is round. In the West, we tend to call this type the "moon face." This sort of face is traditionally said to be pale or drained of color, which is often indicative of poor circulation. The eyes (in common with the ruling element) can be watery.

People with water faces tend to lack self-confidence and be dependent on others for reassurance and support. If they find themselves alone for any length of time, they will tend to prevaricate, putting off decisions for as long as possible. This may be why people with water faces are often accused of being lazy. It is true that they tend to lack energy and often become tired and lethargic, but that is not quite the same thing. The lack of physical energy is made up for by an abundance of vivid imagination. They have a rich and rare fantasy world that is often a more comfortable place to inhabit than the real one! On the other hand, this vivid imagination can give rise to unrealistic expectations, disappointments, and possibly hypochondria.

## The Volcano Face

The volcano face is a variant of the true fire face, but in practice, it is found far more often. The volcano is also triangular in general outline, but more generally resembles a truncated pyramid, flattening at the forehead. This type of face tends to be bony, with very little softness about it. The complexion is sallow, and the person often possesses quite a lot of moles. In common with the true fire face, it is doubtful that the volcano type was blessed with a happy childhood. There is likely to be considerable resentment seething beneath the surface, and this can provide the impetus for this person to make great strides, develop big ambitions, and generally deal with the world on his own terms. Deep and thoughtful, he nevertheless can deal with others as long as they do not cross him, and is possessed of a strong sex drive. However, there is far more self-control than the fire type, and annoyance is more likely to be expressed through bitter words and sarcasm rather than through outbursts of violence. This self-control gives another clue to this character because he is solitary by preference, may be considered eccentric and prone to unusual notions, and has very individual hobbies and enthusiasms.

## The Bucket Face

The bucket face is not strictly a true elemental type. It is a variant on the metal type of face. Its shape is the opposite of the volcano face, a truncated triangle that is widest at the top, descending to a flattened chin. Possessors of the bucket face are artistic because, as well as being influenced by the hard determination of metal, they are also in tune with the softer qualities of water. This type has many varied interests. They are intelligent, perceptive, and witty and are fast learners. Not as cool and cunning as those of true metal type, a person with a bucket face may be easily hurt and can be overly sensitive and acutely aware of another's pain.

This friendly, outgoing personality wants others to love him and to approve of him. He wants to experience life to the fullest, meet all kinds of people from all occupations, and enjoy their company in their surroundings, but on his own terms. He may learn some hard lessons this way because there are those who will take advantage of this person's goodwill. Another common feature with the bucket face type is a tendency to marry young. This is because in early life he yearned for emotional security.

# The
# Brow

3

The forehead or brow is the solitary feature of the heavenly or celestial zone of the face. It is also symbolized as one of the prominent features or "five mountains" of the face. Its symbolic animal is the phoenix, otherwise called the red bird of the south, and the entire area is governed by the fire element of Chinese tradition. This fiery aspect represents the intellectual capabilities and the processes of thought. The Chinese consider the height and breadth of the forehead as well as any distinguishing features, such as the hairline, and the grooves and wrinkles that may be found upon it, to have a direct bearing on intelligence and the capacity to learn.

In terms of age, the brow is associated with youthfulness. The central area just above the hairline corresponds to the fourteenth year. It is home to five of the significant age positions, namely fifteen, eighteen, twenty-one, twenty-four, and twenty-seven. The other age positions dealing with the teens and early twenties are found dotted about all over the brow area.

## The Three Regions of the Brow

As well as indicators shown by the hairline, along with the height and the width of the forehead, there is another factor to consider on the celestial area of the face. This is the division of the brow into three horizontal zones relating to specific mental functions. The topmost of these zones, nearest to the hairline, is dedicated to the imagination. The middle area represents the faculty of memory, while the lower zone, found just above the line of the eyebrows, symbolizes the powers of observation.

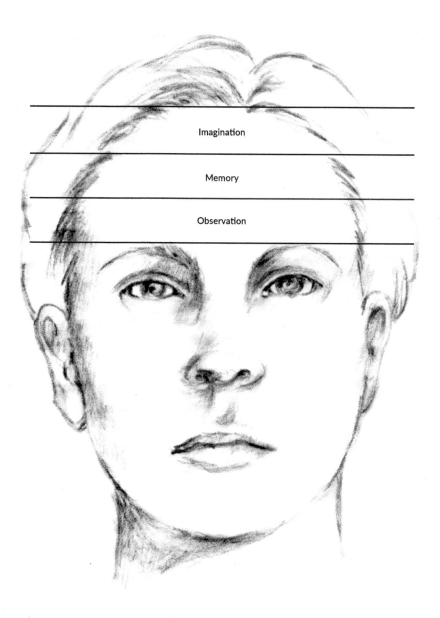

Imagination

Memory

Observation

The three regions of the brow

Any prominence, bulge, scar, or mark in one of these three areas will reveal problems or advantages connected to the mental faculties of imagination, memory, or observation. Should the area above the eyebrows be more prominent than any other segment of the forehead, the perceptive abilities will be emphasized. A brow that bulges in the middle will point to an exceptional memory, while one that protrudes at the top just beneath the hairline will indicate a vivid imagination and may show a potential for exaggeration and fantasy.

## The Hairline

Any hairline can be even or uneven. If it is even, the person is likely to be one who keeps to the straight and narrow and who will not step outside the conventions of his society. However, if the hair growth is uneven, then the outlook on life is likely to be far more rebellious. Therefore, it is equally likely that the views, beliefs, and actions of this person will often be at odds with conventional opinions.

### Receding Hairlines

Male hairlines in particular are subject to recession, so when assessing the shape of the hair growth, it is important not to overestimate the height of the forehead. Loss of hair does not increase the height of the forehead, so if you examine the forehead closely, you will be able to detect the original hairline.

# The Shape of the Hairline

In common with the face as a whole, the shape of the hairline falls into five basic categories that are associated with the five elements of Chinese tradition.

## The Long, Straight Hairline

This feature is often found on a person with a square, earthy type of face or a rectangular, wood face. Most often, it indicates a rational and methodical person. Straightforward and conventional, people with this style of hair growth can be somewhat unimaginative and plodding.

## The Short, Straight Hairline

Often found on people with one of the metal faces, it is similar to the longer version above. However, these people are rather self-obsessed and they tend to repress their desires. Consequently, they may be irritable and they may possess narrow, moralistic views. It may point to an unhappy childhood and a need for appreciation and affection. It is also likely that such a person is prone to anxiety, or they could be quite promiscuous.

## The Rounded Hairline

This is a watery hair-growth pattern and, in common with that changeable element, its possessor may be fickle. If it is connected to the water face shape, then its possessor is likely to

be superstitious and overly imaginative. If this hairline is combined with a face shape other than water, it is more positive, because then it indicates a powerful intuition and a more open expression of feeling.

### The Peaked Hairline

A hairline that rises to a point toward the crown of the head is associated with fire, and this signifies great ambition and a desire to rise to exalted heights. This person will have great intelligence but may be markedly intolerant of other people's views and remarkably fixed in his own. It may also reveal that this person wishes to put a lot of distance between himself and his origins and to re-create his life in a new, more satisfying form.

### The Widow's Peak

The M shape of the downward-pointed hairline is associated with the wood element. The possessor of a widow's peak does not like to be responsible for other people, and many with this feature prefer to live alone. This sort of hairline reveals someone who is very gifted but prone to self-doubt, and it can indicate a rather sensitive and creative nature. Although usually shy, the owner of this hairline often desires public acclaim. On the other hand, it may also hint at a superior attitude, self-indulgence, vanity, and in some cases narcissism.

## The Height of the Forehead

Popular folklore has it that the height of the forehead is the main indicator of intelligence. The practitioners of Chinese face reading share this common view and add that forehead height is usually an indicator of wit. Therefore, a person with a prominent and noticeable forehead is automatically considered cleverer than a person whose brow is low. This belief gives rise to the description of an intellectual as "highbrow."

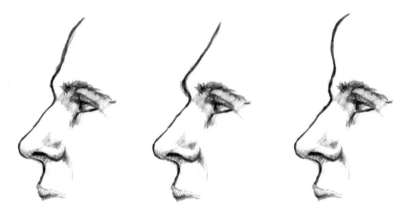

Height of the forehead: standard, low, and high

The height of the forehead should be measured from the point between the eyebrows to the hairline. Classical proportions have it that this distance should be equal to the length of the nose and the distance from the tip of the nose to the tip of the chin. If, however, the height of the forehead is smaller than either of those, it reveals a lack of intelligence, forethought, and charisma. It may also point to a lack of social skills. Working and social relationships may be punctuated by heated disagreements.

## The Width of the Forehead

This distance is measured from temple to temple in a line that is about an inch above the eyebrow line. The distance across the forehead is symbolic of the breadth of vision. Thus, if the forehead is broad, the mind is open to new concepts. Should the forehead be narrow, then its possessor's vision will likewise be limited, and this indicates a person blinded by ironclad preconceptions, prejudices, and intolerance.

## The Seven Horizontal Creases

The horizontal creases on the brow can provide even more information. Strictly speaking, Chinese face reading does not often take notice of these, but this is not the case in the Western art of physiognomy. According to this discipline, the lines of the brow reveal the image and the impact that one will make on society.

There are seven possible creases to be found on the forehead, and these are symbolized by the seven traditional planets of astrology. The highest crease is said to have the dour nature of pessimistic Saturn; the one immediately below it has the optimistic nature of expansive Jupiter. The warlike Mars follows, with the central brow line below that. The central line is associated with the Sun and shows how strongly personal identity is felt. Amorous Venus, eloquent Mercury, and the domestically inclined Moon creases are found below the line of the Sun, in that order.

In practice, it is difficult to spot which of the planetary lines are present. Some people have a smooth brow with no creases at all. This could be taken as a sign of a distinct lack of character. Having all seven is not a good omen either, because it indicates a confused and melancholy nature. The best omen is the presence of just three distinct parallel creases. These are known as "Three Fortunes" and are said to grant good luck, an advantageous start in life, and a prosperous old age.

One well-defined horizontal crease straight across the middle of the forehead is a good indicator of a life filled with remarkable achievements. This is the Sun line. The fortunate possessor of such a well-defined Sun line will be a person who enjoys a good reputation, and in some cases, there is at least the possibility of fame. The central line also indicates an optimistic person blessed with abundant energy and a strong constitution.

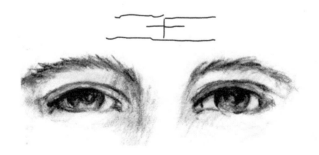

If the dominant crease occurs closer to the eyebrows, then it is likely that it is the line of Mercury. This is not quite as good a feature to possess as the Sun line, but it does reveal cleverness, swiftness of thought, and an eloquent and witty personality.

If any of the horizontal creases of the forehead are scarred, blemished, frayed, broken, or very faint, then misfortune is present. The fortunes are marred in one of the three zones of imagination, memory, or observation. This, of course, depends on the zone of the brow in which the damaged lines are found.

## The Vertical Creases

Much emphasis is placed on the vertical creases rising from the top of the nose because they are said to be very significant in revealing the course of an individual's fate.

### The Hanging Needle

The hanging needle is the name given to a solitary central line rising from the top of the nose. It is considered a generally good sign, signifying great powers of concentration. This character will rise to a prominent position through diligence, persistence, and

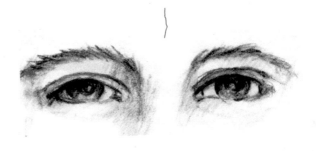

vision. It is unfortunate that this feature can also indicate selfish-ness, anxiety, and a tendency to make enemies who will cause him financial problems. However, if another line branches off from the hanging needle, then the outlook becomes much more positive and fortunate. Should the hanging needle be crossed by transverse lines, this person is far too single-minded, often to the point of ruthlessness, and may be prone to violent outbursts.

## Parallel Creases

Two vertical creases rising parallel to each other is a feature found on people who are well balanced. It indicates one who is willing to listen to both sides of an argument and to give impartial judg-ments. However, the type, shape, and inclination of these creases can affect the interpretation.

## Inward-Sloping Creases

When parallel creases incline toward each other, it reveals a self-centered character, although without the ruthless single-mindedness that goes with a single line. It is likely that this person will have relationship difficulties simply because he is too selfish to accommodate the desires of a partner.

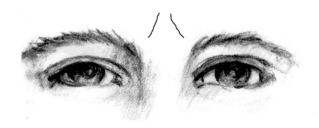

### Inverted Creases

Vertical creases that incline toward each other and then bend back on themselves suggest that the subject lacks the courage of his convictions. It indicates a person who is anxious and lacking in confidence.

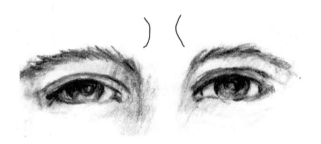

### Meandering River Creases

Meandering parallel creases reveal a person plagued by uncertainty and lack of purpose. The unfortunate owner of this feature will find it difficult to find a lasting role, and he may wander aimlessly from job to job, and relationship to relationship. Tradition states that this is a very unlucky brow feature, indicating a person who finds himself in considerable peril.

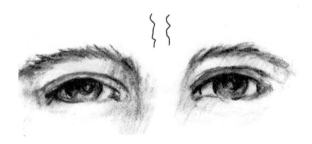

## Crossed Vertical Creases

Parallel creases that are crossed by transverse lines show an irritable, tense character. Those with this feature are often frustrated and sad people who find themselves unable to sustain a worthwhile relationship.

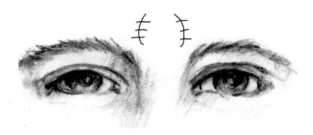

## Broken Vertical Creases

If the vertical creases appear to be nothing more than a collection of short lines progressing up the forehead, it is not good news for this person—especially in the third decade of life. This need not necessarily be a disastrous factor, but a character-building experience. Any misfortunes that occur in the subject's twenties are likely to be rectified in later life.

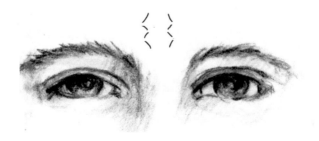

### Three Vertical Creases

If three parallel vertical creases are found, this person will be very fortunate and he will rise to a position of honor and authority. In some cases, the three creases indicate fame. This suggests that this person will be influential and that he will benefit from his celebrity.

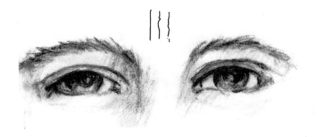

### Trident-Like Creases

When the two outer lines of a three-crease formation turn away from each other, it is a generally fortunate feature, but can be spoiled by some rude, peevish, and self-indulgent character traits.

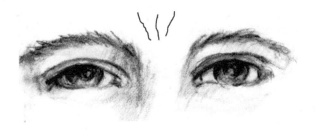

## Three Broken, Wavering Creases

When the vertical creases are both broken and wavering, it is taken to be a very bad sign. Traditionally, this feature indicates a criminal temperament. It certainly shows a ruthless nature and a readiness to gain advantage by dishonest means.

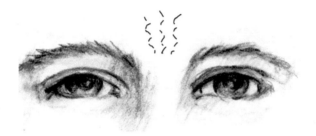

## Four or More Vertical Creases

Many vertical creases are not considered a favorable omen, even if they happen to be well formed, straight, and unblemished. This is an indication of a total lack of direction and severe restlessness that allows no peace of mind. While it is true that the possessor of this feature will be blessed with many talents, he will rarely finish anything and will waste his efforts on frivolous and unrealistic endeavors. This feature is often associated with the destructive effects of alcohol or drug abuse.

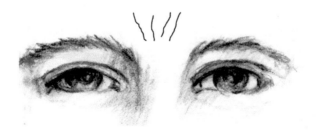

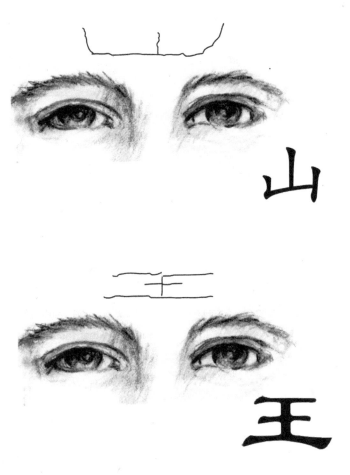

Chinese ideogram symbols

## Chinese Symbols on the Brow

Certain Chinese symbols have their place in this ancient art—although to be frank, the chance of finding a combination of vertical and horizontal grooves that form one of these patterns on the brow is slim. The first formation resembles the Chinese character for "king," while the second symbolizes "mountain." If you do find such a person, he is marked by destiny. He will be loved and respected by his family and friends, and even strangers will take to him easily. He will achieve prominence and prosperity and may even leave a unique mark on history.

# The
# Eyes

4

The eyes are regarded as the windows of the soul. They are the first features to capture our attention, as they depict the real person gazing out through the mask of the face. The eyes alone remain much the same throughout life, whereas the nose, ears, hairline, and mouth are subject to change through growth and aging.

In the age position chart of face reading, the eyes signify the mid- to late thirties. The inner whites of the eyes relate to age thirty-four on the left and age thirty-five on the right. The left pupil correlates to age thirty-six, while the right relates to age thirty-seven. The outer whites represent age thirty-eight on the left and age thirty-nine on the right.

In terms of the Palaces of Fortune, the area above each eye is the *T'ien Chai Kung*, the Palace of House and Farm. The area below each eye is the *Nun Nu Kung*, the Palace of Man and Woman. These palaces deal with family relationships and domestic issues.

## General Characteristics ·

The eye is interpreted according to its position, clarity, and overall shape. The "ideal" type of eye should have a large iris, but not so large that it almost covers the whites. On the other hand, an iris that is too small suggests that the individual is accident-prone and constantly in trouble through no fault of his own.

Eyes should not be bloodshot or have prominent blood vessels. In addition, the eyes should not bulge out too much or habitually look angry. The general rule says that the brighter the pupil is, the better it is.

If the eyes are dull or dominated by low, heavy eyebrows, this is compared to thick clouds obscuring the light of the moon. This

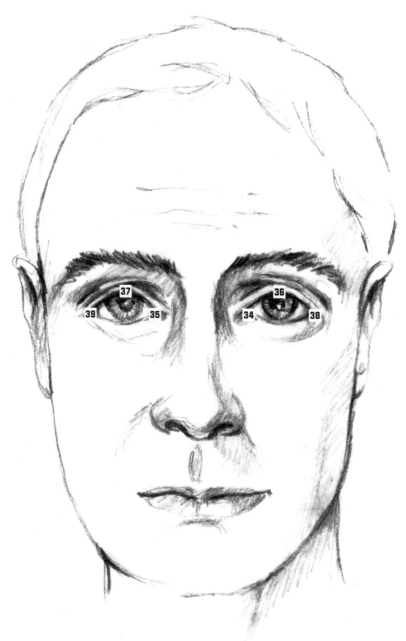

Age positions of the eyes

Eyes beneath heavy brows

combination of features reveals a character that plans everything but is concerned too much with detail. This person will rarely put his schemes into action. It may also show an individual who promises much but delivers little.

Big, wide eyes that look surprised suggest a happy-go-lucky, approachable person who is nevertheless a shrewd businessperson. Deep, dark eyes reveal artistic talents and intense emotions. Eyes that protrude or are very round and staring belong to a hard worker who has experienced misfortune. This is a generally unlucky person who will have to work very hard to achieve any success. Adequately spaced, well-shaped eyes show a flirtatious nature and a strong sex drive.

A person who holds your gaze with his own is honest and reliable. This is the mark of a forthright but reasonable person. This individual is open-minded and magnanimous.

If someone raises his eyes while speaking, then he is very opinionated, obstinate, and pompous. He is always ready to give you the benefit of his views, whether you want to hear them or not.

A person with quick, darting eyes has numerous ideas, plans, and desires. However, he is easily bored, has little staying power, and finds it difficult to concentrate on anything for long.

A careful calculator will look you up and down while you are speaking. This marks a subtle, shrewd, and cunning pragmatist who is slightly shady.

## The Slope of the Eye

The inclination or slope of the eye is also considered important. The eyes should ideally lie along a horizontal plane, but in some cases, they will incline upward or downward. The more pronounced the upward slope, the more the character will be extroverted, confident, proud, and strong-willed.

A downward slope tends to create a sad impression. However, this mournful look is deceptive, and in reality, this person is usually cheerful even though he is thoughtful and introverted.

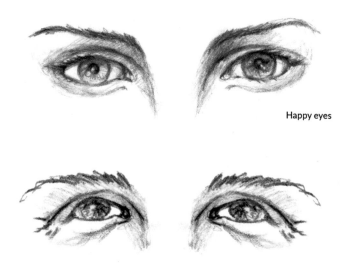

Happy eyes

Sad eyes

Sympathetic, affectionate, and kind, this person will enjoy a long and happy emotional relationship.

## Crow's Feet

We in the West tend to be rather concerned by the appearance of age marks or crow's-feet around the eyes, but the Eastern viewpoint is quite different. If the person is over forty years of age, then small wrinkles, or crow's-feet, around the eyes (especially at the outside edge) are a normal sign of aging. If, however the person is youthful, then the appearance of crow's-feet takes on an extra significance. Traditionally, according to the age positions of the face, the area at the outer edge of the eye relates to the twenty-eighth year on the right and the twenty-ninth on the left.

Four or fewer narrow wrinkles at the edge of the eye can be a general indicator of the course of luck throughout life. This type of person is good to have on your side in difficult situations. This subject has remarkable organizational abilities as well as being someone who revels in challenges.

Wrinkles that incline upward are considered a very auspicious sign, foretelling good fortune and happiness in relationships. However, a downward inclination of wrinkles suggests less harmonious relationships, work difficulties, and financial problems.

The worst scenario is when the crow's-feet have a scissors-like appearance, crossing over each other in opposite directions so that some go upward and some downward. This person is very stubborn, refusing to accept advice or admit to mistakes. This individual's life is fraught with emotional turmoil. It is also

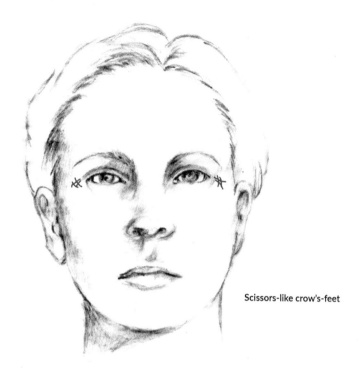

Scissors-like crow's-feet

probable that he is a complainer, often creating a dispute over nothing.

Noticeably long crow's-feet reveal problems with commitment and a lustful nature. Possessors of long crow's-feet are likely to have a series of unsatisfactory relationships. Particularly long wrinkles may also indicate a lazy person who is willing to live off the efforts of someone else. He loves a life of luxury but is unwilling to work for it.

Although the appearance of four wrinkles at the outer edge of the eye is normal, the presence of many lines suggests that this is a lonely person. If this feature occurs in a young person, the crow's-feet suggest lethargy and lack of purpose.

## The Upper Eyelids

A fold on the upper eyelid suggests a person who shows great self-control. If there is no fold, then there is an overly emotional nature and a tendency to overreact.

Eyelids that droop in the middle are found on untrustworthy people who are preoccupied with seduction. A drooping eyelid denotes someone who is cunning, self-serving, and without conscience.

A fold on the upper eyelid

No fold on the upper eyelid

## The Lower Eyelids

If the red inner surface of the lower eyelid is visible, it can reveal a wanton and lustful nature, especially in women. In men, it can suggest impotence or at least sexual insecurity.

# The Traditional Types of Eye

There are many different types of eye shape, depending on the surrounding features of the eyeball and the position of the iris itself. These features have suitably poetic (and frequently unflattering) descriptive names relating to their interpretation.

## The Three-White Eye

This type of eye has the iris at the bottom of the eye, with the white to the left, right, and above. This sig-

nifies a determined and confident person who is very truthful, somewhat forthright, and often tactless. He is strong-willed, often has a foul temper, and is easily frustrated by the slow actions and apparent inefficiency of others.

## The Wolf's Eye

The wolf's eye describes the iris floating just under the upper eyelid, with the white to the left, right, and below. This is the mark of a shrewd and ruthless person. He knows exactly what he wants and how to get it! Traditionally, this shape

is an indicator of cruelty or at least a tendency to ignore other people's feelings. This is no stranger to conflict and thrives on challenges. If you look at photographs of serial killers or other sociopaths, they often have this kind of eye.

## The Four-White Eye

This type of eye has the iris set in the very middle of the eyeball. The white surrounds it on all sides, and it is often found in eyes that are prominent or bulge. This type of person is very adaptable and accustomed to the unexpected. However, he is prone to furious outbursts when his desires are unfulfilled. This type of person always has a plan, usually several. It is when all of the plans fail that the fireworks begin. If a person's eyes suddenly develop a lot of white around them, the subject is probably suffering from an overactive thyroid.

## The Triangular Eye

The upper eyelid has a distinct raised portion in the middle. The color of the iris tends to be strong, and its surroundings are somewhat off-white. A strong eyebrow usually accompanies this type

of eye. This is a sure sign of great achievement. Owners of this eye are competitive and they thrive on challenge. They are observant and possess excellent judgment. They know when to act and when to be passive. The triangular eye is said to be the mark of a natural politician, although some would say he is a plotter. It is certain that he will make the most out of all opportunities and gain wealth and status.

## The Angry Eye

The angry eye is recognized by concentric circles within the iris. This type of eye is also known as the wheel eye. This individual is very physical. This active individual prefers to be practical rather than to spend time thinking. He may lack foresight and can cause chaos if he is not properly guided. It is unfortunate that the possessor of the angry eye won't even notice the havoc he leaves in his wake. Needless to say, he is constantly offending someone.

## The Fire Wheel Eye

The description of the fire wheel eye is one of the few occasions in face reading that iris color is mentioned. The iris has a green, red, or blue ring around it, and there are concentric circles of color within the iris itself. This eye indicates a volatile temperament. This person exists in a state bordering on fury, and he frequently explodes over minor issues. It might be said that he is always on the lookout for someone or something to be

offended by! He is extremely alert, overly critical, and possibly a little paranoid, always assessing the strengths and weaknesses of those around him.

## The Sand Eye

The sand eye is notable for the flecks of yellowish color within the iris. In the West, the sand eye is very common in those with blue or even lighter eyes. This is a mentally acute and perceptive person. He is a great communicator—quick thinking, quick talking, and never short of an answer. He loves an argument because he possesses an innate capacity to spot all flaws in his opponent and run rings around him with devastating wit. He loves doing this so much that he is in danger of becoming quarrelsome if he does not exercise self-control.

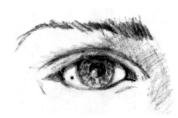

## The Mole Eye

The mole eye has a small spot of dark color in the white of the eye. The possessor of this type of eye is likely to have periods of good fortune, but they will not last. It is likely that people who take advantage of his good nature will contribute to his misfortunes. He does not deserve this treatment, because he has a kind heart, but unless he is extremely careful, his own charitable disposition can lead him to ruin.

## The Drunken Eye

This type is similar to the four-white eye because the iris is found low on the eyeball. In this case, the area surrounding the iris will tend to be reddish or yellowish rather than white. These eyes have heavy upper eyelids and tend to look lethargic. Any crow's-feet will be made up of many short wrinkles.

The name of this type of eye is not an indication of drunkenness! In fact, this person will be very sexy and literally have a "roving eye." He is usually charismatic and extremely attractive to the opposite sex. However, this feature indicates a life filled with many good and bad events. There will be times when a series of mishaps in life will cause all his plans to fail. On the other hand, there will be periods when the opposite is the case and absolutely everything will go right. When you spot this feature, do not expect consistency.

## The Unwrinkled Eye

This type of eye has few or no wrinkles around it, even when the possessor is in middle or old age. It is smooth and rounded at the edges, having no angles at all in its outer portion. This eye suggests youthfulness and an active mind. This person's powers of persuasion could lead him into a career as a salesperson, public relations expert, or spokesperson. However, this very eloquence could also get him into trouble. The romantic life is problematic because this persuasive ability is very seductive. A person with an unwrinkled eye is easily tempted off the straight and narrow path of fidelity. He is likely to have many serial relationships but is also capable of concurrent ones.

### The Pea Blossom Eye

This eye is very long, inclining upward into a bow shape in the middle. Both the iris and the white of the eye are somewhat cloudy or shadowed. This is the mark of a very cautious person. He is perceptive, and he is a keen observer of human nature who may be cynical. This trait is likely to be completely concealed by his charm. Those with pea blossom eyes will rarely look straight at you while they are trying to work out your motives. This type is often extremely talented. These people often excel in the arts or in careers that require charisma and flair. They are also very popular, with many lifelong friends and an active social life. Some of his old friends will be old lovers because those with pea blossom eyes can retain affection even when passion has faded.

### The Elephant Eye

This eye will tend to be narrow and long, giving an impression of wisdom. It has many wrinkles both above and below the eye. This person gains by experience: he is perceptive, he has a good memory, and he is compassionate and helpful to those in need. He will go to great lengths to give assistance to anyone who has stirred his sympathies. This type of person is sensitive, creative, enthusiastic, and full of humor.

## The Lion Eye

The iris is high, similar in form to the wolf's eye, but there will be few or no lines on the lower eyelid and several strong lines on the upper. The gaze of a person with the eyes of a lion is brave, direct, and unflinching. This person has flawless judgment, and others will admire him and see him as an example and role model. He is respectable and responsible. Most often he is so career-minded and determined that his

diligence and ambition will bring great reward. He takes his role in life very seriously indeed and cannot tolerate being the butt of jokes or even bear lighthearted banter.

## The Tiger Eye

Very similar to the lion eye, the eyes of the tiger are more golden. The crow's-feet at the edge will be short, faint, and rather scattered. There are few or no creases beneath the eye, but one strong line on the upper eyelid. This is a forceful character with strong attitudes and opinions. Other people will look to this person for guidance and leadership. However, he is a loner who is happy in his own company, with an occasional pressing need for soli-

tude. It is likely that at times he will work or live alone. He may be considered eccentric, as he could choose an unusual lifestyle.

### The Crane Eye

This type has a central iris and is big, rounded, long, and noted for clarity. There may be two or more creases on the upper eyelid. The crane eye shows that its possessor is likely to be generally lucky through life and that he will win steadfast and loyal friends. He is deeply compassionate and loves nature. This is a person of unimpeachable integrity. The honesty is such that this person will speak openly and be very forthright because he cannot stand any sort of deviousness.

### The Eagle Eye

Eagle eyes are long and fairly narrow. The iris is high on the eyeball, which possesses a yellowish tinge. One long crease is usually visible on the upper eyelid, but beneath, there are no wrinkles at all. This is a solitary sort of person. By his own choice, he will

prefer to live or work alone. He sees the world his own individual way, and he will live life on his own terms. These people do not take kindly to being told what to do at any time. Although he is fond of family and friends, he tends to think, "Absence makes the heart grow fonder," and keeps them at arm's length. This fierce independence means that he will not ask for help under any circumstances.

### The Goose Eye

This type of eye is fairly long but is so well rounded it appears to be in perfect proportion. The iris is centrally placed and may possess a golden hue. There are definite creases both above and below the eye. This is a relaxed personality with a light-hearted view of life and an easy, outgoing personality. This person makes friends easily, and if in the course of events some fall by the wayside, so what?—he can always make more. This is not an ambitious person, because he will tend to be happy the way things are. Although people with goose eyes are not high fliers, they will have contented and fulfilling lives.

### The Swallow Eye

These are deep-set eyes framed by a long crease both above and below. The eyes are bright and clear, giving the impression of sharpness. The swallow eye is elegant and rather beautiful. This extremely trustworthy person firmly believes that a promise is a sacred trust. He will gain admiration for the way he keeps his word, even when breaking it would be in his best interest. It is unfortunate that the swallow eye does not indicate wealth or status, but it does reveal a comfortable and fulfilling lifestyle.

### The Horse Eye

This type of eye is watery and bulges slightly. There are many folds of skin and creases on the lower eyelid, but the upper lid is generally free of wrinkles with a soft and delicate appearance. Crow's-feet at the outer edge of the eye will be inclined downward. This person is a hard worker who carries on through thick and thin. He may struggle against overwhelming odds. Like a cart horse, he will diligently persevere with his thankless tasks through all weathers and in all conditions. It is unfortunate that this person may not receive his just reward for all his efforts. The horse eye reveals a person who will have more than his fair share of difficulties. Despite this, he does not lose heart, and his courage will put charismatic people to shame.

### The Lamb Eye

Lamb eyes are dark with a yellowish tinge to both the iris and the whites. There may be concentric lines within the pupil. The upper eyelid will have folds of skin while the lower eyelid will

not. In addition, the lower eyelid will be flat and have thin, delicate skin marked with fine lines. Any crow's-feet will be thin, faint, and scattered. This individual is dutiful and always busy, a hard worker who rarely feels he has the time to enjoy the results of his efforts. People who possess lamb eyes have to rely on themselves because they learn early on in life that there is no point in relying on anyone else. This person is constantly in demand, but it will not matter how overloaded his schedule is; there is always just enough time for one more task.

## The Ox Eye

This is a large, rounded eye, but it is not bulging. The iris and the whites are very clear indeed. This is a very forgiving person who will overlook past wrongs and give those who offended him a second or even third chance to put things right. He is gentle in attitude and outward manner. This person's feelings run very deep indeed, but it is not part of his character to express himself in anything other than a calm manner. The crow's-feet take on an extra signifi-

cance with ox eyes. An upward inclination reveals an extremely trustworthy nature. This person will never let you down. The downward inclination of the eyes denotes a nature that is too passive, so this is one who wants an easy life and who will make empty promises to keep it that way.

## The Pig Eye

The pig eye possesses heavy, coarse lids, and the eye is dark and muddy. The eyes are relatively small and tend to peer suspiciously about them. This is not a lucky eye shape. Pig eyes reveal a tempestuous and irritable, sharp-tongued and impulsive person. There is a self-esteem prob-

lem here, as this person is very insecure. He conceals his weak self-image behind a barrage of constant and often inaccurate criticisms of others. Those with pig eyes make enemies very easily and unnecessarily. If such a person would hold back his opinions and think before he speaks, his life would be much more pleasant.

### The Monkey Eye

The monkey eye has an iris that lies toward the top of the eye. The eye is small and fairly short in length. There is a crease or fold on the upper eyelid, and the fold curves down sharply toward the outer corner of the eye and possibly even beyond it. This is an inquisitive person who is capable of mastering a multiplicity of skills. This subject is optimistic and outgoing, with great courage. He is also bright, inventive, and cheerful, and he will gain the admiration of those who are not so brash. The ancient Chinese firmly believed that those with monkey eyes delight in eating fruit.

## Eye Color

Among the people of China and the oriental races of the surrounding areas, an iris of dark brown to black hue is usual; therefore, eye color never became an important factor in Chinese face reading. However, Western face readers developed a system of classifying eye color due to the variety of eye colors present in peoples of European descent. Here are the Western eye color ideas:

- Those with hazel eyes are emotional and warm and possess a keen intellect.

- People with ordinary brown eyes appear to be extroverted and excitable but actually are conservative and cautious beneath the surface. It is said that they are less sensitive to pain than those with lighter eyes.

- Blue eyes can vary greatly in color, from deep azure or sapphire to pale, watery blue. Tradition has it that the greater the depth of color, the greater the passions will be.

- Those possessing blue eyes are calmer and more compassionate than those with brown eyes.

- People with very pale eyes can be extremely shrewd and calculating, while those with deep blue eyes like a quiet life and are more passive.

- True gray eyes are a rare feature. This lack of color denotes a lack of ability to make decisions, even though it also reveals a logical, emotionally controlled nature.

- People with green eyes are daring individuals who are inventive and cheerful.

# The
# Eyebrows

5

The eyebrows are one of the five prominent features described in Chinese face reading. They conveniently provide the border between the upper or celestial zone and the central zone of self-will. When we relate the eyebrows to the age positions that are dotted around the face, we find that these features correspond to the early thirties. The outer ends of the right and left eyebrows correspond to ages thirty and thirty-one, respectively, while the end nearest the top of the nose relates to ages thirty-two on the right and thirty-three on the left.

The eyebrows are very revealing of emotional states. They are the most mobile features of the face and are the most expressive of both character and changes of mood. Without the clues provided by the eyebrows, it is almost impossible to deduce emotional states or mental attitudes. Those people who lack eyebrows—perhaps having shaved them off—are therefore enigmatic characters who like to create an aura of mystery.

## The Prominent Eyebrow Ridge

A well-defined and prominent eyebrow ridge reveals a courageous and individualistic personality. Those who possess this feature are usually obstinate, and they are always convinced that they are in the right—especially when they are totally in the wrong! This sort of person can expect many long, drawn-out disputes. More positively, this character is a crusader and an asset to any cause that he champions. The prominent eyebrow ridge also denotes excellent powers of concentration.

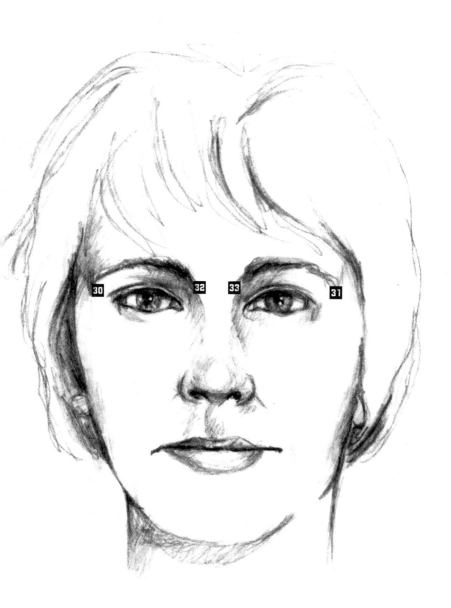

Age positions of the eyebrows

# Eyebrow Growth

### Upward-Growing Eyebrow Hairs

It is a dangerous sign if the hairs on the eyebrows have a noticeable upward growth pattern, because although it reveals bravery, it also indicates a foul and volatile temper. This person is very tactless, often forcefully speaking before he thinks and acting without any forethought or consideration of consequences.

### Downward-Growing Eyebrow Hairs

When the hairs of the eyebrow noticeably grow downward, the person lacks confidence. These people are often nervous and will attempt to avoid confrontations at any cost. There is also a refusal to accept blame for any mistakes or wrongdoing and an equal refusal to face the consequences of their own actions. This is a person who has little self-esteem and relies on his loved ones too much.

### Eyebrows with Mixed Growth

In this type of eyebrow, the hairs at the top of the eyebrow grow downward while those at the base grow in an upward direction. The traditional name for this sort of feature is "hairs that embrace," or rather charmingly, "cuddling hairs." This is revealing of an anxious person, an unnecessary worrier who is plagued by negative thoughts.

## Scattered Directions of Hair Growth

This feature is generally found in thick eye-
brows where all the hair grows in different
directions. Often this is the mark of the self-
made man. He will have to cope with unexpected difficulties and setbacks throughout
life. Possessors of this type of eyebrow
may not have much help or acceptance by
those in positions of power and authority, but they will progress
through their own efforts.

## Delicate Eyebrows

Slim, delicate eyebrows reveal a calm, placid,
and untroubled character. These people like
a quiet, undemanding life, but when duty
calls, they have the ability to cope with anything they are called upon to do with speed
and efficiency.

# The Twenty-One Shapes of the Eyebrow

Ancient Chinese tradition defines many different shapes of eyebrow, although for general purposes, we can content ourselves with defining twenty-one basic shapes.

## The Long Eyebrow

This type of eyebrow has a gentle curve and extends beyond the edge of the eye. It may extend beyond both sides of the eye, and

in some cases, these eyebrows also meet in the middle of the forehead. Even though there is a common belief that one should never trust someone whose eyebrows meet in the middle, the long eyebrow actually reveals an active intellect, considerable wit, and eloquence. It predicts a happy and prosperous middle age.

## The Short Eyebrow

The hairs on this type of eyebrow tend to be rather coarse and uneven in length. This eyebrow does not extend to the full length

of the eye. This feature could indicate an unhappy childhood, possibly someone who comes from a fairly small family or one who has little contact with his relatives. His family relationships may have been soured by arguments and resentment. He may have lost touch with his close relatives due to circumstances beyond his control.

### The Big Eyebrow

The big eyebrow extends the full length of
the eye and is wide with strong hair growth.
Those possessing a wide eyebrow are never
afraid to speak up or to make their feelings
known. This person will invariably be the
dominant partner in all his relationships. If

the big eyebrow is found in conjunction with a prominent brow
ridge, this person will be a very formidable individual indeed.

### The Clannish Eyebrow

This type of eyebrow is said to resemble
the Chinese character for the number one.
The most notable feature is that the hair
roots are visible in this type. There is thick
hair growth, and the eyebrow is of medium
length, but it should extend a little beyond
the edge of the eye. The clannish eyebrow

reveals a love of family, and it may indicate a large, extended clan.
The owner of this eyebrow will have an excellent reputation and
a long, stable, loving marriage.

### The Loner Eyebrow

The shape of this eyebrow resembles the
letter Y or the Chinese character for eight.
There is sparse hair growth in a generally
thin eyebrow. As the name implies, this feature is found on people who prefer solitude

and who are ill at ease in company. This is a dedicated individual and a hard worker who enjoys his job. It is considered a fortunate eyebrow, since it predicts a long life and much contentment.

## The Ghost Eyebrow

The ghost eyebrow is similar to the loner type but is more curved and descends lower, to the bridge of the nose. An upward hair growth is usual. This person does not trust others and he plays his own cards close to his chest. His true thoughts and feelings are concealed. He may be resentful and rather antagonistic.

## The Rolling Eyebrow

In the rolling eyebrow, the hairs are thick and curly, usually inclining toward the outer edge of the eye. This unusual feature denotes a capacity to take control and for others to accept his leadership. Eyebrows of this type are often found on the features seen on the faces of politicians, military leaders, and business magnates.

### The Broom Eyebrow

The broom eyebrow is long and thick, with wild, scattered hair growth toward the outer edge. The wildness of the hair growth reflects the wildness of the person who possesses it. He is a supreme individualist who requires great understanding within his close relationships. It is likely that he comes from a large family, but it is unlikely that he keeps in close contact with them. The broom eyebrow does not promise great prosperity, but on the other hand, its owner will never be short of money.

### The Little Broom Eyebrow

Identical in form to the broom eyebrow, this type is equally wild but shorter, rarely extending to the edge of the eye. This feature depicts an impatient and temperamental person who is adept at talking himself into trouble and equally skilled at talking his way out of it again. This person is difficult to live with, and his problems most likely stem from a difficult family background.

### The Beautiful Eyebrow

The hairs of beautiful eyebrows grow upward, and they are fine, rather long, and delicately curved. The eyebrow may curve very high or rather low, but either way, it is always described as being elegant and refined. It denotes an honorable person who is noted for trustworthiness. This person has excellent judgment, and he will always keep his word. He is wise and a skilled diplomat who is much sought after as an arbitrator in all disputes. The beautiful eyebrow is considered very lucky.

### The Mortal Eyebrow

The hairs of the mortal eyebrow are coarse and bushy. The eyebrow is very short, wide, and thick. This person enjoys being sociable and having close friends and lasting relationships, but he prefers to live alone because he feels a need for his own private space. He may be estranged from his parents and the rest of the family, and he may feel let down by them. Traditionally, this type of eyebrow predicts that he will have children in later life.

### The Sword Eyebrow

The sword eyebrow is located high on the brow and is flat, long, straight, and wide—becoming thicker at the outside edge. All the hairs will tend to grow in the same upward direction. The possessor of this eyebrow is wise and very astute. This is a natural leader, and this feature is often found on those who are successful in business. The sword eyebrow is considered fortunate, indicating longevity and a large family.

### The Knife Eyebrow

The hairs of the knife eyebrow are usually coarse, while its shape suggests a dagger blade. This eyebrow indicates a cunning person, one who is quick on the uptake, who is astute, and who will gain great advantages throughout life. However, there is a certain

laziness here, because this individual will always seek the easy route to his goal. His type of eyebrow is also taken as a sign of a boaster.

### The Rising Eyebrow

To recognize this eyebrow type, all you have to do is think about *Star Trek's* Mr. Spock and you can't go wrong. The rising eyebrow is shaped like the knife and sword types, but in this case, it rises diagonally from the bridge of the nose. A person with this feature has great determination, and he refuses

to admit defeat in any circumstances. He is extremely dominant and can be argumentative and aggressive when he sets out to get his own way. Early successes are usual with this type, and he makes achievements throughout life, but personal and family relationships may suffer due to this relentless ambition.

## The Weeping Eyebrow

The opposite of the rising eyebrow is the weeping eyebrow. It also has a diagonal slope, but in this case it falls downward and makes its possessor look sad or mournful. It is difficult to work out what the possessor of this eyebrow thinks or feels because he makes a virtue of being enigmatic. This person is fast-thinking and very clever. He will not be afraid to offend or take advantage of others if that is the quickest way to the top. This is a shrewd individual, quick on the uptake, and ready to make the most of all his opportunities.

## The Willow Leaf Eyebrow

The poetically named willow leaf eyebrow is curved and delicate, with tangled hair. It belongs to a person who is open, honest, and friendly. He has an excellent intellect and a lively mind. He loves social life and he is extremely popular. He will make influential friends who will help him achieve success. Those who possess willow leaf eyebrows do not usually start a family until later in life.

### The New Moon Eyebrow

The new moon eyebrow is set high above the eye, gently curving into a crescent shape. True to poetic form, the hairs of this eyebrow are fine and glossy, as if filled with an inner light. They all grow in the same direction. The possessor of this eyebrow is compassionate and thoughtful. He is honest

and trustworthy in all his dealings. This is a sure sign of fidelity in relationships, and it is considered fortunate for both early and later life. His dealings with his family are likely to be fulfilling, too.

### The Longevity Eyebrow

This eyebrow is noticeably wide, with a significant lengthening of the hair at the tail end. Often these end hairs will curve downward beyond the edge of the eye. The hairs are usually glossy and dark. The possessor of this eyebrow is very fortunate, as he is likely to enjoy a long, happy, and successful life. This type of eyebrow denotes someone

who is creatively gifted and a good writer and fluent speaker. Noted for friendliness and charm, this person is very attractive and alluring.

### The Dragon Eyebrow

The dragon eyebrow is well shaped and elegant, with fine, glossy hair. It rises in a straight diagonal line for most of its length and then slopes downward past the outer edge of the eye. The dragon eyebrow is an indicator of wealth. The family of origin is likely to be large and to have spread out over a wide area. The owner of this type of eyebrow is ingenious, with a good instinct for business. His friends and associates respect him. He loathes injustice of any kind, and he is not afraid to speak up on a point of principle.

### The Silkworm Eyebrow

This type of eyebrow gently rises on the forehead. The silkworm eyebrow is smooth, with an even shape rising gently on the forehead. Its hairs are smooth, silky, and somewhat curled. This eyebrow points to someone who is popular and trustworthy. He is self-disciplined, quick-witted, and capable of making the best out of any situation. The silkworm eyebrow is very lucky, often predicting fame and fortune.

## The Lion Eyebrow

The lion eyebrow is wide, thick, and curly all along its curving length. Its roots will be visible even though the hair is dense. This type of eyebrow is indicative of a strong constitution, and it predicts longevity. The shape of the lion eyebrow can give its possessor a look of constant irritation, but it masks a generous spirit, thoughtfulness, and an affectionate nature. However, even though this is a person who will win the respect and admiration of others, his domestic life is not so happy. There may be marital difficulties and domestic tension.

# The
# Nose and
# Cheekbones

**6**

In Chinese tradition, the nose is either regarded as the "emperor of the face" or thought of as the "fifth mountain." This is the most central and most prominent feature, which, in common with all middles and centers in oriental belief, is symbolic of the earth element. The Chinese consider the cheekbones as sentinels, guards, or mandarins standing to attention on either side of their emperor. They also call the cheekbones "the Mountains of the Green Dragon and the White Tiger," and these animals are symbolic of the elements of wood and metal, respectively. The wood element is located on the right, and the metal element on the left. The brow and the chin represent the remaining two elements.

As far as the age positions of the face are concerned, the cheekbones represent ages fifty-eight on the right and fifty-nine on the left.

The cheekbones are said to support the nose; therefore, they should incline toward the nose. Flat or hollow cheekbones do not perform this function, and the influence of the nose area is therefore weakened.

If either cheekbone is higher or more prominent than the other, then the interpretation of the nose loses much of its importance. This is particularly true if the left cheek is higher than the right. This asymmetric feature will increase a person's caution to the point of cowardice. A person with this feature is likely to do very little with his life simply because he does not dare to take any chances at all.

Should the nose be small and flat while the cheekbones protrude, tradition holds that "the emperor is a puppet of his ministers." A person with this feature is likely to be gullible and easily led.

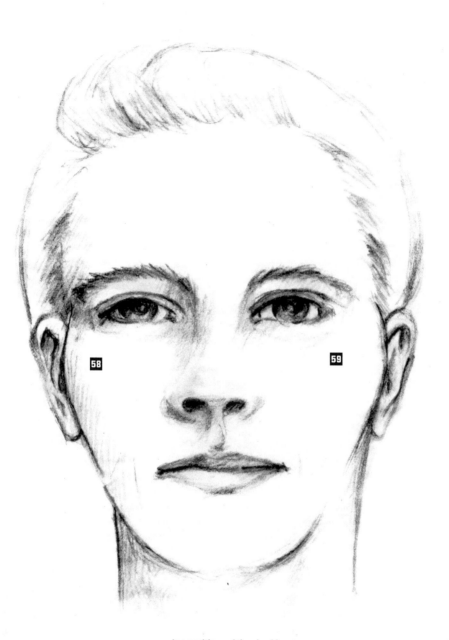

Age positions of the cheekbones

Protruding cheekbones combined with very taut skin are not a very fortunate feature and are said to be a sign of bad luck. This person may be a spendthrift with no thought of the future, or he will constantly find himself prevented from taking advantage of the opportunities that are presented to him. Even if he does prosper at one or more periods in his life, the trend will not last long and he is likely to lose his gains as quickly as he obtains them.

Flat or dented cheekbones reveal a shy person with little self-esteem. This sort of person wants a quiet life with no complications and studiously avoids responsibility.

## The Divisions of the Nose

The nose is divided into six areas, each related to one of the age positions of the face and each described by a traditional Chinese name. The right nostril is called *t'ing wei*, while the left is known as *lan t'ai*. The tip of the nose is *chun t'ou*, and at eye level we find the *shan ken*. Between them on the bridge of the nose lie the *nien shang*, which is found at the end of the nasal bone, and the *shou shang*, located on the cartilage.

Four of these points are significant positions. These are the shan ken, relating to age forty; the nien shang, relating to age forty-three; the shou shang, relating to age forty-four; and the chun t'ou, at the tip, relating to age forty-seven. The nostrils correspond to age forty-eight on the right and age forty-nine on the left (see the illustration of the age positions of the nose on the next page).

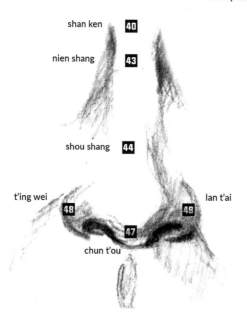

The divisions of the nose, and corresponding ages

shan ken **40**

nien shang **43**

shou shang **44**

t'ing wei **48**

lan t'ai **49**

**47**

chun t'ou

A lump on either the shou shang (age forty-four) or nien shang (age forty-three) indicates an eccentric and unpredictable nature. A person with either feature will have difficulty in relating to others and will experience communication problems and the resultant problems in maintaining relationships.

## The Central Mountain, Emperor of the Face

Proportion is one of the most important factors to consider in Chinese face reading, so ideally the nose should not be too large or too small, too thin or too wide, in comparison with other features of the face. As usual, the complexion of the nose should ideally be clear, while the tip of the nose should be reasonably rounded and not too bulbous.

If it is possible (in Caucasian faces) to see into the nostrils when the face is viewed straight on, then this person is likely to be extravagant, with no true sense of value or of money. This is someone who can see no reason why he should listen to advice. He is convinced he always knows best and will do exactly as he likes. This is a very unfortunate feature, forecasting a life full of regret.

Narrow and rounded nostrils

Oval-shaped nostrils reveal an astute nature. There will be an essentially cautious, prudent nature and a dislike of taking risks. This is someone who is financially shrewd and bound to prosper.

Very rounded nostrils indicate a perfectionist who likes a life of order and system. He is an organizer by nature and is happy to organize others as well as himself.

## General Characteristics of the Nose

Although a long nose is regarded as preferable to one that is short, this is only the case if it is in proportion to other features and does not dominate the face. A nose that is thin and pointed reveals an independent person. He may be a loner who is inwardly shy yet prefers not to show it. He may feel awkward in the company of relative strangers and possess few true friends.

A very large nose, either in length or in width, found in combination with flat, sunken, or insignificant cheekbones, is a warning of recurring troubles within the family and reveals relationships that are fraught with problems.

A very thin, beaklike nose placed high at the center of the face is a sure indicator of a lover of luxuries who can rarely afford his lifestyle.

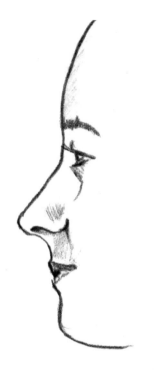

Thin, pointed nose

A thin nose that starts high on the face with a noticeable (but not too prominent) nose bone shows a decisive nature, the ability to make quick, correct decisions, and the determination to carry them out.

If the bones that make up the structure of the nose are plainly visible, this depicts a willful, rather arrogant person who hates

Above: Plump nose

Below: Uneven nostrils

to be corrected, to be contradicted, or to accept advice. However, this person is not a fighter, and he will tend to withdraw from conflicts rather than engage in a struggle.

A plump nose tip combined with wide nostrils is a sure indication of a very strong sex drive.

A sympathetic, loving, and warm nature is revealed by a soft, rounded nose. There is an overall softness about this compassionate character. This person is open and generous with good advice and with his money, but he may be taken advantage of by "hard-nosed" individuals.

A reddish-tinted thin nose says that this person is not clever with cash and that he is constantly in debt.

One nostril that is higher than the other indicates a sharp, incisive person. This perceptive soul is very shrewd and rather cunning. He may lack conscience, and he will be quick to take advantage of opportunities.

A noticeably pale nose, possibly having a grayish tint, reveals an active mind that is constantly filled with plans. This "ideas man" will not give in even when the odds are stacked against him. If anyone can find a solution to the most intractable problem, this is the person!

# The Profile of the Nose

Now we look at the nose in profile—that is, sideways on.

## The Sword Nose

This nose type is long, sharp, and pointed. It is generally bony and hard to the touch. This is not an easy person to get to know. He appears aloof and unapproachable, but in reality he is shy. Yet underneath this natural reserve, he is a compassionate soul. His early family relationships will have been turbulent, and there may be unresolved issues concerning his birth or childhood. He is naturally conservative, so he may take his time in adapting to new situations but will have a successful life. One of the best examples of a sword nose is found in portraits of Napoleon Bonaparte.

## The Lonely Mountain Nose

The lonely mountain is notable for a high nose tip. The cheekbones and the middle portion of the nose (nien shang and shou shang) will be flat. Although this character will live a comfortable life, he will be forced to settle for less than he would really like. Difficult experiences in his early life convince him that he must be self-reliant, despite the fact that family and friends want to help him when times are hard. It is likely that he is too proud to accept this

assistance or others are not in a position to offer it. The owner of the lonely mountain nose will not achieve his highest ambitions but will nevertheless contrive a comfortable lifestyle and be generally happy with his lot in life.

## The Hairy Nose

The nostrils of this type of nose are particularly large, open, and hairy. The body of the nose will be thick and strong, but the very tip will be rather thin and flat.

This is a competitive and financially lucky person. Often a spendthrift, he tends to think of his resources in terms of "easy come, easy go." A natural gambler, his resilience will stand him in good stead in good times and bad. This person does not despair. He will achieve success, not once but many times—he will find that his life is a roller-coaster ride of difficulties.

## The Bun-Bridge Nose

The bridge of this type of nose bulges outward, giving a mistaken impression of bulk, when actually the body of the nose is rather slim. This is a good-humored and popular person. However, he does tend to be erratic and lack consistency. He will experience highs and lows with money matters, friendships, and close relationships, which go through marked phases. Different people will fulfill necessary roles in this person's life at differing times. However, this character is extremely courageous and a consummate survivor.

## The Three-Bends Nose

The very top of the nose (the shan ken) is a deep hollow. The bridge of the nose bulges, while the tip is sharp, thin, and rather pointed. This character's life will never be boring. It is a good thing that he is resilient and that he learns how to handle the twists and turns in his fortunes. He may find himself at the top of the professional tree, only for a branch to break when he least expects it. Conversely, at the lowest points in life, unexpected opportunities and good fortune will suddenly occur, thus lifting him from a rut.

## The Collapsed Nose

The bridge of this type of nose is-dented or hollow. A nose that gently curves inward from top to tip can be regarded as a form of collapsed nose. This feature indicates a person who is shrewd and selfish. Always on the lookout for an opportunity, he has an eye for the big chance and a quick profit. In life's game, this is a winner, even if his ideas are a little too ambitious to be practical. He may not achieve as much as he desires, yet he should do reasonably well in material gains. This character avoids responsibilities and is adept at escaping trouble.

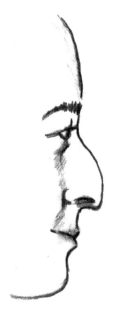

### The Eagle-Beak Nose

As the name implies, this type of nose resembles the beak of a bird of prey. It is hooked and sharp, curving outward from the top. This character is self-confident and quite formidable, and he puts his own interests first. Intolerant and impatient by nature, he relishes a challenge and will rarely avoid arguments or be daunted by large projects. He tends to make his own opportunities because he cannot be bothered to wait for the right moment and will pre-empt a situation and head directly for his goal. He is probably quite ruthless.

### The Protruding-Nostril Nose

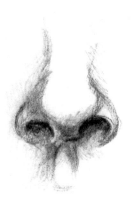

This nose is on the large side, with a rounded, slightly upturned tip, and one can see both nostrils when looking directly at the face. This type of character takes changes of fortune in his stride. He is easygoing both with people and with money. When he has money, he will spend freely and be more than generous to all around him. However, when his cash resources are lean, he will be dignified, rarely if ever complaining about his poverty.

## The Knot Nose

The knot nose can be any shape, its defining feature being a protruding lump on the bridge of the nose, particularly situated on the nien shang. This powerful person thinks he knows best in all circumstances. This person would rather accept failure than act on the advice of someone else. On a more positive note, he is generous and good-hearted and will gain true friends and allies throughout his life.

## The Unbalanced Nose

As the name suggests, one side of the nose is noticeably higher than the other. This is an unfortunate feature indicating the loss of a great deal of money, missed opportunities, and disappointment. However, if the tip of the nose is rounded, the interpretation is somewhat better, mitigating the losses and adding luck when it is most needed. This person will become a philosopher and will gain great wisdom through his difficulties.

### The Philosopher's Son Nose

This type of nose has clear skin and is either straight or slightly curved. The philosopher's son nose tends to be rather long, well balanced, and somewhat pointed at the tip. The top of the nose is rather wide. This may look like an aristocratic nose, but this person is not snobbish in the slightest. On the contrary, he is egalitarian and open-minded. This is a lover of life who treats everyone with equal respect. He also possesses a strong moral sense and will be prepared to defend a point of principle to the hilt.

### The Lamb Nose

The lamb nose is straight and quite strong for most of its length, but the tip becomes rounded or even bulbous and the nostrils are clearly visible from the front. This is a hardworking individual who will achieve success through persistent effort. Very energetic and ambitious, he will gain respect for his determination. Although he will achieve career success, his relentless drive could possibly harm his personal relationships. His is also an unforgiving nature, prone to harboring deep resentment if he feels he has been wronged.

## The Deer Nose

This nose has the appearance of being rounded yet strong. The tip particularly is softened yet slightly protruding. The bridge of the nose may curve slightly inward. This individual is a great friend to others, and he supports those who need help. He believes that a promise is a sacred trust. He is faithful and loyal, and he will stand by family, friends, and colleagues through thick and thin. He also has an instinctive ability to choose his friends well, and he tends to surround himself with the right people. The deer nose is a fortunate feature, indicating longevity and probably a large extended family.

# The
# Ears

# 7

An individual's ears are unique, and they are considered singularly important. Before the development of the use of fingerprinting, criminals were often identified by their ear shapes. In face reading, however, the shape and relative positions of the ears have much to do with an assessment of a person's intelligence. The ears have great importance. In many ways, the ears are the most private area of the face. This is emphasized by the fact that certain hairstyles hide these revealing features. After all, one really has to express a great deal of trust to allow an intimate examination of one's ears.

The first thing to assess concerning the ears is their positioning relative to the eyebrows and the tip of the nose. It is also important to notice whether the ears are set far back on the head or in a more forward position, closer to the cheekbones.

## Position of the Ear

To determine the precise angle of the ears, one must imagine a line starting at the eyebrows (the border between the celestial and human levels of the face) and then continuing through the ear hole itself to the back of the head. According to the rules of Chinese face reading, the farther back the ears are on the head, the more intelligent the person is likely to be. It is normal to find that the ear is set two-thirds of the way back from the eyebrows, indicating an average intellect. By the same logic, if the ear is very close to the cheekbones, then the chances of this person being rather dim is increased.

# Length of the Ear

The length of the ear is also considered an indicator of intelligence. Should the ear tips rise above the eyebrow line while the lobes extend lower than the tip of the nose, then this could be taken as a mark of genius. Most people have an average intellect and they have ears that are found within these parameters. Remember that the ears are not the only indicators of an individual's brain capacity. The height and breadth of the brow is also a factor, as much as the length and angle of the ear.

It is quite common to find a person whose ears extend above the level of the eyebrow line while the lobe is also at a higher level than the nose tip. This individual is likely to be lively and an extrovert and a natural entertainer. This person loves to be the center of attention. He is an original thinker who has unconventional working methods. He wins both admiration and criticism equally throughout his life.

Ear tips that are positioned lower than the eyebrow line while the rest of the ear is long, with the lobe reaching the level of the tip of the nose, reveals a lack of attention to detail. This person is a daydreamer and time waster who is neglectful of duties. This situation is made worse if the ear is soft, fleshy, and rounded.

When the ear tips extend above eyebrow level, while the lobe, or ear pearl, is on exactly the same level as the nose tip, the person has a persistent and determined nature. This individual will gain success through hard work. This feature also shows good fortune, artistic talent, and a creative mind.

Ears of different lengths or indeed of different sizes are considered a bad sign, indicating misfortune. Plans will rarely come to a successful conclusion, and those with this unlucky feature will be compelled to take second best and to make unwelcome compromises.

## Other Ear Features

Small ears indicate a delicate constitution and are the mark of a worrier. A person with this feature should concentrate on the here and now rather than fretting over what might be. It is worth bearing in mind that some races tend to have smaller ears than others do, so the Chinese ideas of large and small might not always apply in our modern homogeneous society.

Ears that stick out indicate a great thinker who usually "lives in his head," often giving the impression that he is from a different planet entirely! This can also be taken as a sign of skepticism. This is often an indication of someone who was an insecure child, and this early anxiety may remain a persistent trait throughout life.

Ears that are particularly prominent, often cruelly described as "jug ears," are usually a sign of a turbulent early life. The frustrations and repression created by this troublesome past will tend to stay with this person, but they may be channeled into positive directions later on in life.

Ears that lie relatively flat to the head indicate excellent judgment. This character will patiently listen to all sides of an argument and make his decisions in a cool frame of mind. This feature reveals both a happy childhood and a contented and prosperous middle age.

Pointed ears reveal a suspicious person with a sharp perception. This person is very critical and possibly aggressive. They see negativity in others and they can be prone to the feeling that everyone is out to get them.

## The Symbolic Structure of the Ears

Traditionally, the outline of the ear is called the "great wheel." This great wheel is divided into three smaller wheels, mirroring the basic threefold division of the face. The upper portion of the ear is called the "heaven wheel"; the middle part, the "human wheel"; and the lobe, or "ear pearl," is also called the "earth wheel." In addition to this, the interior of the ear (around the ear hole) is also called the "inner wheel." The very center point is the ear hole itself, which symbolically connects the outside world to the inner workings of the brain.

## The Ears and Childhood

According to the facial age positions, the ears represent early life. The ears reflect the impressionable and receptive period of childhood. Beginning at the top and descending to the lobe, the left ear covers ages zero to seven, while the right deals with the eighth to fourteenth years.

# Ear Coloration

The color of the ears adds even more information to the interpretations of their positions, prominence, and shape.

An ear that is red or pink is another indicator of a lively mind. An individual with red ears can absorb information easily and quickly. This shrewd person is capable of using information to his best advantage. Ears that are very red show a stressed person who would benefit from meditation and cutting down on caffeine and other stimulants.

If the reddish tint is so strong that the ears appear to be purple, then this indicates poor circulation and delicate health. Perhaps cutting down on sugar and alcohol might help.

Grayish ears indicate a talkative person. If this skin coloration is found on small ears, this denotes an indiscrete person who finds it impossible to keep a secret, even when revealing what he knows is likely to go against his own best interests. Should gray areas suddenly appear on the ears, tradition states that an unlucky period is about to occur. Stoic patience is advised until this episode is over.

Pale ears that are whiter than the rest of the skin show that this person will be extremely successful in life. It can be taken as an indicator of fame, and it is certain that this individual will gain a great reputation.

## Traditional Types of Ear

In common with the other facial features, such as eyes, eyebrows, and nose, the tradition of face reading gives extra meaning to the various types of ears.

In many ways, the ears echo the face as a whole, so the first five types of ear are named after the five elements of oriental mysticism—wood, fire, earth, metal, and water.

### The Wood Ear

The topmost area of this type of ear slopes upward and is larger than the middle area. The inner ring grows beyond the outer wheel. The ear is thin and there is either a small lobe or no lobe at all.

This person will have a patient and persistent nature. Good fortune will not come to him easily, and he will have to persevere to make a success of life. However, no matter how many trials and tribulations he experiences, he will achieve his desires in the end. This type of ear predicts a happy, healthy, and prosperous old age. However, if this ear type is combined with a face shape that is metal or earth in nature, the chances of this happy fate are reduced.

### The Fire Ear

The top of the heaven wheel is pointed. Like the wood ear, the inner ring extends beyond the outer wheel. The fire ear is hard to the touch and not fleshy, but it has a lobe. This ear belongs to an extremely headstrong and independent person who finds it almost impossible to accept criticism or advice. He is impatient, fiery by nature, and not likely to be an intellectual. This person demands action, and he will  sulk when he does not get his own way. If this ear type is combined with a fire face shape, then there is more chance of a fulfilling, happy life.

### The Earth Ear

The earth ear is comparatively large, fat, and fleshy. The lobe is full and rounded, as indeed are both the outer and inner rings. The outer ring particularly will make up a large percentage of the ear itself. This ear is considered a good omen because it signifies a long, happy, and prosperous life. This person is extremely loyal to his friends and family, and he feels that the happiness of others is every bit as important as his own happiness is. He will be 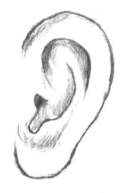 greatly loved and respected. The outlook is not quite so lucky if the earth ear is found in conjunction with wood-type facial shape.

### The Metal Ear

This ear is quite angular, with a hard lobe. Its color is paler than the skin of the rest of the face. The upper portion of the ear rises higher than the eyebrow line, and the outer and inner rings are so close that they almost touch. This ear indicates an active intellect, curiosity, and perception. The metal ear is associated with creative talents, and it predicts career success and wealth. However, it can also denote selfishness, an individual in pursuit of his own personal gain who will sacrifice personal relationships to get it. Difficult family relationships may be indicated. If combined with a wood type of face shape, the metal ear foretells bad luck.

### The Water Ear

The Water ear is thick and soft, with a large, rounded lobe. It is set close to the head, rising above the eyebrow line, and will tend to be lighter in color than the rest of the face. This type of ear belongs to a good negotiator, who is very clever, quick-witted, intelligent, and calm. This person is cool in a crisis, maintaining his placid exterior through thick and thin. He will inevitably do well in business. However, should the water ear be combined with a face shape that is fire in nature, the individual can expect sudden misfortunes and financial losses.

## The Chess Ear

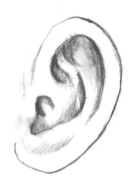

The chess ear is quite small and well rounded. It is firm to the touch and quite thick. The chess ear is paler in color than the rest of the face and rises above the eyebrow line. This person is a strategist, and as the name implies, he is good at games of skill. This person loves a challenge, and his determination ensures that he will never give up a struggle if there is the slightest chance that he can win. In his life, as in the games he plays, he is brave and enterprising. Chess ears foretell great successes and joy in the middle years of life. If chess ears are found with a metal type of face, then happy, lasting relationships are predicted. It is not so lucky if they are found with a wood type of face.

## The Touching-Shoulder Ear

The touching-shoulder ear is also described as the royal ear and most descriptively as the very long ear. This ear rises above the eyebrow line and reaches below the tip of the nose. The lobe is thick, pendulous, and rounded. The ancient Chinese approved of people with this feature. It is often depicted in images of the Buddha and is traditionally associated with gravity and an authoritative manner. This person will be wise and competent and will achieve great things in life. He is likely to be dedicated and capable of long periods of sustained effort to reach his ambitious goals. There is very little that such a person cannot achieve once he puts his mind to it.

### The Catching-Wind Ear

This ear is wide and rounded, with emphasis on both the upper and middle wheels. It is very prominent, extending outward from the head, so it is adept at "catching wind." The catching-wind ear is a type that sticks out from the head, and it is likely that it denotes an unhappy childhood. There is the likelihood of an unsettled background, with the possibility of estrangement from the parents. This person will have known periods of isolation, and he may have left home early. He makes his own way in the world, and he is ambitious and a hard worker. Once he has chosen his goal, he will achieve it against all odds. Even so, he feels the need for a faithful partner to make him secure.

### The Upper-Forward Ear

The upper-forward ear can be recognized by its S shape. The top of the ear slopes toward the eyebrow and sticks out somewhat. The lobe slopes toward the back of the head. The lines of the inner and outer wheels are indistinct, merging into each other. This feature reveals someone who has a great deal of pride and who is extremely independent. This character is self-reliant and solitary by nature and prefers to work through his concerns in solitude. He is slow and painstaking, and it takes a long time for him to build trust in anyone else. This person's solitary preferences can cause problems if taken too far, and in the end he may suffer due to his isolation.

## The Pig Ear

This type of ear is quite undefined, almost being a sort of indistinct fleshy appendage on the side of the head. It is usually thick and soft, resembling the "cauliflower ear" associated with aging boxers. It does not have distinct inner or outer wheels. These ears belong to an impetuous, aggressive person who is easily goaded into rash behavior. This person is often insecure and indecisive, with many inner frustrations that easily boil over into outbursts of hot temper. In financial terms, this person should, surprisingly, do quite well, although he is not careful or wise with his money.

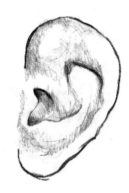

## The Tiger Ear

The tiger ear does not stick out. In fact, one of the main definitions of the tiger ear is that it clings tightly to the side of the head. This ear type is small, firm, and thick to the touch, with an outer ring that is tightly curled. The lines of the outer and inner wheels are indistinct, being broken or uneven, and melting into each other. This is an honest, straightforward person, sometimes to the point of being painfully forthright. However, even his straight talking will win admirers who appreciate his candor. The possessor of tiger ears is impressive, showing all the qualities of leadership, but he may be tactless. He is decisive, and once he has made up his mind he will be firm and he will get on with things.

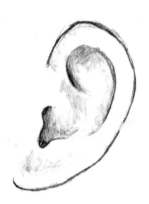

### The Rat Ear

This is a small ear, rarely rising above the eyebrow line. It is full and rounded, with a tightly curled outer wheel. In contrast to the West, where the rat is seen as a filthy denizen of the sewers, in China the rat is a symbol of prosperity and financial acumen. Possessors of rat ears are certainly very astute. This observant person is quick to take advantage of any opportunity to make a profit. He is also willful and determined to get his own way, but he is in no hurry to do so. His deceptively casual manner conceals a cool, calculating mind. The actions of this person will rarely be spontaneous, because he works out his strategies long in advance.

### The Porcupine Ear

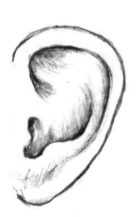

Contrary to what one might expect, this type of ear is not spiny! The upper wheel of the porcupine ear is very wide, and it rises above the eyebrow line. The rest of the ear is firm to the touch and quite straight. Chinese tradition describes the porcupine ear as having a "strong appearance." People with these ears demand respect and have "prickly" personalities. This sort of person can be rather cynical, but he is an excellent, if rather cutting, judge of character. He is an original thinker who possesses great vision, but he is not clever with money. This restless subject will find it difficult to settle down. In Chinese superstition, a porcupine must be pampered, or misfortune in the form of plagues and natural disasters will inevitably follow. The same might be said for those with porcupine ears.

# Cheek Lines
## of the Face

**8**

The cheek lines are the two creases running from the nose toward the outer corners of the mouth. In the art of Chinese face reading, these lines are referred to as the *fa ling*. According to the rules of this ancient practice, the direction and shape of these lines can say a lot about the nature and character of the subject.

According to the age positions of the face, the fa ling lines link to the mid-fifties, with the left side corresponding to fifty-five years of age and the right to fifty-six.

## The Parallel Lines of Fa Ling

If the two lines of fa ling are parallel on both sides of the mouth, or if there is a branch line running from either of the cheek lines, it is suggested that the subject may suffer from a great deal of stress in relation to finances. Though the subject should find it easy to make money or hold down a job, he may find problems with hanging on to money and discover that it flows out of his hands like water.

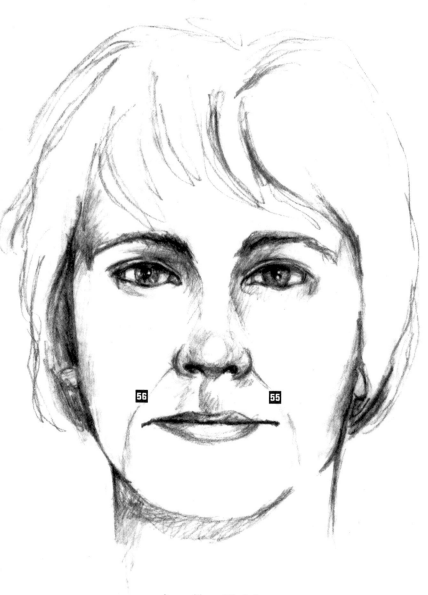

Age positions of the fa ling

## Moles on the Fa Ling

Dark moles or protrusions on either fa ling line suggest that the subject may have a tendency toward extravagant behavior. The subject may find it difficult to put something away for a rainy day, and he may feel the constant need to live for today. This attitude can also extend to the career, and there might be a tendency for the subject to flit from one job to another.

As the fa ling lines refer to the fifty-fifth and fifty-sixth years, a mole on either line could suggest danger for the subject in his mid-fifties. The American president Abraham Lincoln had a mole on his right cheek and was shot dead at the age of fifty-six. Fortunately, the negative effects indicated by moles or protrusions can be neutralized if the subject has a mole or red mark on the tip of his tongue.

## Locking Fa Ling Lines

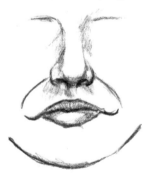

If the subject has cheek lines that join with the outer corners of the mouth, the lines are said to be locking. The ancient Chinese described this feature as "dragons entering the mouth," and it is considered unlucky. The subject might find that he is extremely accident-prone, especially during middle age—but although this looks bad, there is a positive aspect, because he can turn misfortunes around and set himself in a new direction in life.

## Locked and Crossed Fa Ling Lines

Fa ling lines that touch the corners of the mouth and that are crossed by lines running down from the cheeks can suggest that the subject might suffer from stomach problems. The subject should avoid rich foods in an effort to combat potential stomach ulcers or in more extreme cases, food poisoning.

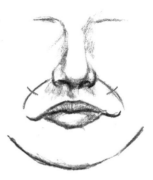

## T'eng Snakes Lines

If the fa ling lines curve toward the mouth but do not touch it, they are known as *t'eng snakes* lines. If they curve outward and down toward the chin, they suggest that the subject has a carefree nature, though in extreme cases this can lead to a reckless attitude toward safety and with regard to personal possessions.

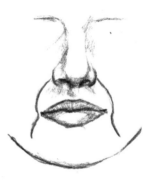

## Broad Fa Ling Lines

Fa ling lines that run down from the cheeks in a broad curve away from the mouth indicate an innovative character, and this can lead to success in business. These lines can also suggest that the subject would be suited to careers involving administration or a job that allows for a creative flare.

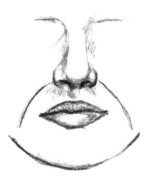

## Long, Thin Fa Ling Lines

Fa ling lines that run sharply down the face, passing the corners of the mouth and possibly bowing in toward the chin, are an extremely good indicator of a long and healthy life. If, on the other hand, the fa ling lines run straight and pass the mouth at a steep angle, this warns that the subject may be his own worst enemy, causing arguments by his outspoken manner and never keeping his word.

## Indistinct or Faint Fa Ling Lines

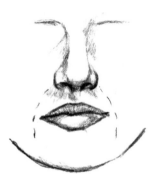

Faint or nonexistent fa ling lines, or lines that break into a myriad of smaller ones, are extremely lucky—but in a very odd way. Although the subject might not have an easy life, the presence of this feature indicates that he always seems to eventually land on his feet. It is true that the subject's own bad judgment lands him in these troublesome situations, and he should be aware that one day his luck might run out!

## Mandarin Fa Ling Lines

Fa ling lines that are deeply creased, and joined both by lines from the corners of the mouth and by lines running up from the chin toward the cheeks, are known as mandarin lines. This feature suggests that the subject is destined to find himself in positions of power and to be able to shoulder a great deal of responsibility.

## Wandering or Unequal Fa Ling Lines

If the fa ling lines are unequal in length or if they wander along different paths from each other, this can indicate that the subject is unstable and lacks a persistent nature. As is common with negatively featured fa ling lines, the subject will find problems around his mid-fifties.

## Upward-Bowing Fa Ling Lines

Fa ling lines that bow predominately upward toward the cheeks are not considered a very good feature. The outlook is bleak, and traditional interpretations suggest that the subject will be plagued with misfortune and ill health.

# The Mouth, Lips, Philtrum, and Chin

9

The size and shape of a subject's mouth denote a great deal about his personality and future prosperity. As with the eyebrows, the mouth can show a vast range of emotions from joy to misery, courage to cowardice, and affection to coolness.

In the art of Chinese face reading, the age ranges of the lips correspond to the early fifties—upper right to fifty-one and upper left to fifty-two. The lower lip corresponds to fifty three on the right and fifty-four on the left, while the midpoint of the lower lip corresponds to the late fifties generally and specifically the fifty-ninth year.

## General Characteristics

Ideally, the lips should be in proportion to the rest of the subject's face, being full and prominent without being too large or too small. Chinese tradition considers it better for a subject to have a large mouth in relation to the overall size of the face rather than a small mouth—as this is said to indicate bad luck.

The size of the mouth and lips should be in proportion, with both upper and lower lips being equal in size. The color is also important, so the lips should ideally be a light red, as this suggests that the subject is honest and well balanced.

The left- and right-hand sides of the mouth should mirror each other, and when the mouth and lips are closed, there should be no gap between the lips. The lips should also be slightly moistened, and if the subject is female, they should be soft without being flabby. A male should have lips that are firm without being too hard.

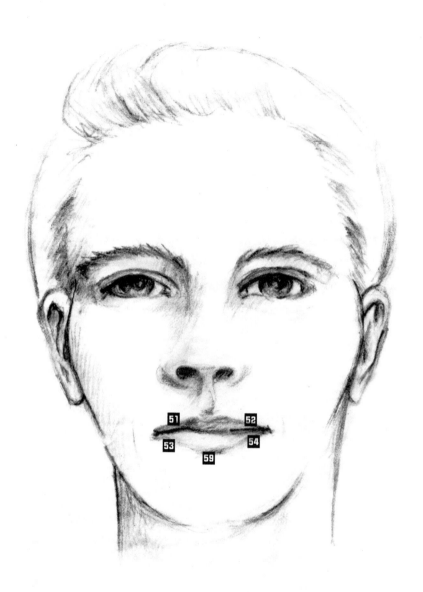

Age positions of the mouth

A perfect mouth

A subject with a perfect mouth is said to be loving, honest, kind, and well respected. A well-formed mouth is said to denote success and good fortune in life, starting in the subject's forties and continuing through the mid-fifties and beyond.

Lips that are full, well balanced, and bright suggest a robust and healthy character with a strong stomach. (The Chinese believed that intelligence resided in the stomach. It was therefore very important, as it was linked to reason and the power of thought.) A subject with this feature will live life to the fullest but may be prone to greed.

## The Wide Mouth

A person with full lips and a wide mouth is more fortunate than one whose mouth and lips are smaller. This person will be popular and the center of attention in any social gathering, although in some cases, this positive characteristic can lead to a boastful person who is prone to exaggeration. He may also be too happy-go-lucky for his own good, lacking any real direction in life. This sort of character also tends to attract the wrong sort of company, much to the disapproval of his family and true friends. It appears that the negative sides of this mouth style are more evident with large-mouthed males than with large-mouthed females. Females with a wide mouth tend to be more fortunate, possessing a very good head for business. Women with this feature may also find success in the entertainment industry.

## The Sea Corners

The edges of the mouth are called sea corners. These can indicate a happy, light-hearted personality when they turn upward and a practi-cal, materialist personality when they turn downward.

Uneven sea corners

A downward turn indicates personal insecurities and anxieties. A subject with a large mouth and sea corners that are unequal or uneven will leap before he looks. This person will never think things through and will always blame others for his own mistakes. The subject may also find that he is always in need of money and that he has a sharp-tongued, bitter attitude because, in his eyes, nothing that goes wrong will ever be his fault.

## The Small Mouth

A subject with a small mouth is said to lack confidence and continu-ally seek approval from others. A small mouth can also indicate a suspicious nature and a certain meanness of character. Thin lips suggest that the subject will have few close relationships and will often be lonely during middle age.

## Straight Line Lips

In Chinese face reading, the way the lips meet is extremely important. If the lips meet in a straight line, then the subject is orderly, logical, and unemotional. This can sometimes have a negative effect on personal relationships.

## A Downward Central Kink

A fairly straight lip with a downward-pointing deviation at the upper midpoint suggests a person who is conventional, stable, and normal. Yet there may be a boiling passion hidden beneath the surface of this average-looking individual.

## Pursed Lips

Lips that purse together when the mouth is closed indicate that the subject is inclined to worry about everything. It can also reveal that the subject has an uncertain temper due to unrealistic expectations of himself and of others.

## The Gently Curved Meeting

Lips that gently meet with a slight upward curve at the sea corners show an individual who is open and friendly, with a strong sense of personal identity. If the lips are also full, the person will have organizational and leadership qualities. When the lips are thick and reddish,

the subject will be flirtatious, sensuous, and prone to finding himself involved in risky personal relationships.

## The Upward-Curving, Uneven Meeting

Lips that meet with a wavering and slight upward curve reveal a personality that is persuasive, eloquent, and creative. This may point to a secretive and scheming nature that is also extremely seductive. This plausible and charming subject never reveals anything truly personal.

## The Very Uneven Meeting

Lips that mirror each other yet meet in an uneven line suggest that the subject will wander off the path of the straight and narrow. This person is isolated and misunderstood. Although

successful in sexual relationships, he may find it difficult to form a lasting relationship because his wandering nature continually leads him astray. The more full the lips, the stronger the sexual desire will be.

## The Open Meeting Lips

Lips that meet while leaving a slight gap denote wit, but this feature can also indicate misfortune in the subject's early fifties. The Chinese philosopher Confucius (Kung Fu Tse) famously had this feature in addition to buckteeth. He lost his favorite son in his fifth decade.

## Traditional Mouth Shapes

In common with other facial features in the ancient art of Chinese face reading, there are various symbolic and unflattering names for the different mouth shapes.

### The Square Mouth

The square mouth has an angular shape and reddish thick lips. A person with this type of mouth is a very lucky individual who finds success and happiness in all areas of life. He is honest, level-headed, and respected.

### The Creative Mouth

The creative mouth has lips that turn slightly upward at the sea corners, giving a smiling appearance. The lips should be thick, reddish in color, slightly moist, and well formed. These traits signal an artistic nature and a good sense of humor, coupled with a clever and straightforward personality. This is a likable and generous individual.

## The New Moon Mouth

As the name suggests, an individual with this shape of mouth may appear to have a permanent smile. This individual will be able to get his point across quite eloquently, with considerable persuasive force. He may also be artistic and be able to concentrate and focus deeply.

## The Fire-Blowing Mouth

This mouth has pursed lips, downturned corners, and a noticeable downward deviation at the upper midpoint. The upper front teeth may protrude slightly and the lips may be rather thin. A subject with this feature will be an individual and a loner. He may have trouble developing long-lasting friendships. Traumatic events in early life may have emotionally scarred him, leaving him feeling resentful and rejected. However, the outlook is not completely negative, because the subject will eventually find soul mates who will contribute emotional security and who will build his confidence.

## The Uneven and Dry Mouth

This type of mouth has dry, dull-colored lips with sharply downward-sloping sea corners and a generally irregular appearance. The subject will stand out from the crowd. He may be unique, which may lead to problems in finding his place in his personal life and career. This could conceivably lead to continual problems with finances, but this unique individual has a patient and determined attitude that will see him through any difficulties. He will also find it difficult to develop trust in others.

### The Fish Mouth

As the name suggests, this type of mouth is quite literally fish-shaped, with noticeably downward-slanting sea corners and thin lips. A subject with this feature will be reliant on others for financial support due to an unconventional lifestyle or prolonged periods of higher education. The subject may spend years seeking a suitable career, but when he finds one, success is sure to follow.

### The Lotus Leaf Mouth

A subject with this feature will have thin, dullcolored lips and a long, slightly downward-curving mouth. This very private person finds it difficult to admit his own faults or even to communicate properly with others. This person may also be a gossip who finds it much easier to talk *about* other people rather than talking *to* them.

### The Unbalanced Mouth

One of the sea corners slopes upward and the other slopes downward, giving the subject's mouth a lopsided appearance. This person has a wagging tongue, but he is also an entertaining and witty individual who embellishes his tall tales. Although this person is outgoing, he is rather insecure, and he uses a barrage of verbal dexterity to disguise this. This mouth is a fortunate feature when it comes to money, but it also suggests that this person tends to live beyond his means.

### The Cherry Mouth

This is the most auspicious type of mouth,
with upward sloping and rounded sea corners, and full, red lips that hide small, white,
perfectly meeting teeth (also known as "pomegranate teeth"). This
person is intelligent, insightful, and wise beyond his years. He will
be helpful, offering useful advice to friends and colleagues. This
individual will find himself in influential company and will prove to
be very influential in his own right.

## The Philtrum

The groove that runs from the middle of the upper lip and connects with the nose is called the philtrum in English and *jen chung*,
or "middle man," in Chinese. In the ancient Chinese art of face
reading, it has a unique importance, as it indicates the longevity
and fertility of a subject. Where the cheekbones were called the
guardsmen, the jen chung is considered the messenger or minis-
ter of the emperor. The jen chung is called the channel directing
the will of the emperor of the face (the nose) to the mouth. This
feature is linked to the age of fifty.

If a male subject has hair growth within the jen chung, this
good omen brings popularity and the ability to make friends. If
there is no hair within the philtrum, the opposite is the case, and
the subject will make many enemies due to an offensive nature.
This will be especially true when the subject reaches his fifties.

### The Deep, Long Philtrum

The long, straight, deep, and broad philtrum is the best type. The subject will have a long, fertile, and fortunate life, and he will see considerable advances in personal status in his fiftieth year; this will continue throughout his fifties.

### The Wide-Based Philtrum

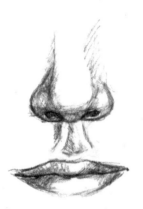

A subject with a philtrum that is wider at the base and narrower at the top is destined to have many offspring. Some sources suggest that the subject may have children in later life and a disproportionate number of them will be girls. According to the views of the founders of Chinese philosophy, this was not a welcome eventuality.

In days gone by, sons and their wives lived with the son's parents and took care of them when they got old, while daughters lived with, worked for, and took care of the parents of their husbands. Although the Chinese preference for sons seems sexist to us, from a practical point of view, sons were a blessing. Daughters were costly to feed, clothe, and accommodate while they were young and of no financial value to their parents in later life. Indeed, if a couple had several daughters and no sons, when they became old, they had to either throw themselves on the mercy of other relatives or starve.

### The Narrow-Based Philtrum

If the jen chung is wider at the top and narrower at the bottom, the Chinese say that "the emperor's message is lost." The physical energy is constricted and the subject will suffer from ill health and low fertility. There will be few offspring, and those that there are will almost certainly be daughters. Yet again, from the ancient Chinese point of view, this is not a fortunate feature.

### The Wide-Midpoint Philtrum

If the widest point of the philtrum is in the midsection, the energy of the emperor's message is constricted; it stagnates and forms a lake. This will reflect on the subject's fiftieth year, indicating depression, illness, and loss.

### The Short Philtrum

The subject with this feature has a noticeably small gap between the upper lip and the nose. Though not conducive to a long life, it does indicate that the subject will have a number of remarkable successes in the time that he has. Alexander the Great had a notably short jen chung, and although he attained much fame and success in conquering most of the known world, he died before his thirty-third year.

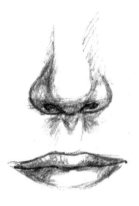

### The Fading Philtrum

This feature describes a philtrum that descends from the nose and fades before reaching the mouth. It is considered extremely unfortunate. Illness, loss, and an early death are indicated, but this becomes less apparent for the subject if the philtrum is noticeably long. A longer philtrum will serve to increase longevity but not happiness, because feelings of isolation and trouble with one's offspring are indicated during later life.

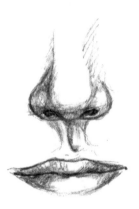

### The Bent Philtrum

A jen chung that inclines to the left or right not only affects the balance of the entire face but also is a bad omen for the subject's life. This feature indicates failure, frustration, and loss of direction, and this may suggest financial problems and depression. It can also indicate that the subject will remain childless.

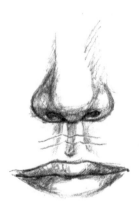

### The Creased Philtrum

If the subject has wrinkles or creases on his philtrum (horizontal or vertical), these are considered a bad sign. If the creases are horizontal, the subject will suffer from business and family problems in his fiftieth year, with the possibility of discontentment in middle age. If on the other hand the creases are vertical, the outlook is better. However, the person may only have children later in life, and men in particular will only father children once they are over fifty. If the subject is female, then she will conceive around the age of forty, and this will be a worrying development. Overall, this type of philtrum is a sign of discontent, discomfort, and worry.

## The Chin

To the ancient Chinese, the chin was thought to resemble the shell of a turtle, and so it was known as the "Mountain of the Black Tortoise." It is also the last of the five "mountains of the face," the others being the nose, the forehead, and the two cheekbones.

The chin is the foremost indicator of a person's willpower. In our modern world, we often use descriptions such as "chinless" or "slack-jawed." We think of the chin and jawline as strong or weak. So even without studying face reading, we make instinctive assumptions about a person based on the shape of his jaw. The jaw can also indicate whether a person is easily tempted. It is linked to a person's sixties and seventies, and so the positive or negative effects of the jaw shape might not show until late in life.

The best shape for the chin is full and fairly broad, but the chin should not stick out as a particularly noticeable facial feature. The chin is a reflection of the jawbone as a whole. For example, a wide, square chin will have a broad jawline. A pointed, narrow chin is normally accompanied by a narrow jawline.

The chin and jaw, like the other features of the face, can be divided into various types for face reading. The main thing to remember is that a broad jawline denotes a determined and strong character.

## The Rounded Chin

A rounded chin is believed to indicate a warm, openhearted, and emotional nature. It also indicates a person who is able to make the best of any situation, who is at ease with himself and the world around him, and who has a charming personality. A longer, more prominent chin belongs to an individual who uses charm to his own advantage—quite literally—winning friends and influencing people.

## The Square Chin

This is the chin shape of a hardworking person, indicating considerable self-will and high achievement. This type of chin describes someone who is honorable, trustworthy, and steadfast in any form of partnership. All dealings will be honest and straightforward. Though the subject may have deep, strong feelings, he might lack charm. If you can accept this, you will find him to be a good person.

Another version of this chin is the dimpled or cleft chin. This person remains youthful even in old age, but he needs to be loved. The famous Hollywood star Kirk Douglas is a classic example, which is not surprising, as this type of chin is also often found on artists and performers.

## The Jutting, Broad Chin

Though similar in meaning to the square chin, this shape of chin extends the qualities of honor and inner strength. Negative qualities of this kind of chin suggest that the subject is a pushy, charismatic flirt and an attractive charmer who is likely to be an unfaithful partner.

## The Pointed, Narrow Chin

An individual with a pointed or narrow chin is considered weak-minded and a less attractive character. Depression, lack of willpower, and unfulfilled dreams will often plague a subject that possesses this type of chin. If this isn't bad enough, the ancient Chinese also believed that a person with a pointed, narrow chin would face troubles in old age. This feature indicates loneliness, betrayal, and a possible short life.

# The Jawline Profile

Look at the profile of the jaw. This rarely changes the interpretations found above, but it is important to consider the distance between the bottom of the ear and the jaw. The most important factor to recognize is the angle and width of the jaw.

### The Angular Jaw

An angular, low jaw stretches away from the ear in shape and at a distinctive angle. A person with this type of jaw is normally very decisive and has strong self-will. If the jaw is also quite broad, then the subject will be a natural leader and will be very commanding, and not take no for an answer. An angular, high jaw is noticeably closer to the ear. Though the subject will still be determined and strong-minded, there is a tendency to be swayed by powerful opinions and to try to please everyone.

Receding chin

### The Curved Jaw

This is the most common jaw shape, and the interpretation of the character type is dependent on the shape of the jaw. If the subject has a receding chin, he lacks self-will and determination. If, on the other hand, he has a stronger, more prominent chin, the determination increases, but with either chin shape, the subject will tend to go with the flow of other people's opinions.

# The Beard

The shape and pattern of beard growth also depicts characteristics. Direction, denseness, and color are the main factors to note here. The main areas associated with beard growth are those of the philtrum, the chin, and along the jawline and above. As has already been mentioned, these areas of the face are linked to specific times of life from the early fifties to the mid-nineties, and the interpretation of the beard is linked to these areas.

## The Most Fortunate Beard Type

The ideal beard is one that is dark in color, with soft, fine, and shiny hair. It should not be too close to the edges of the mouth, and it should leave a narrow line of skin around the lips. A subject with this type of beard is said to be hardworking and honest, with a generous nature. This can also suggest that the subject will be youthful and energetic well into his later years.

## The Thick Beard Type

A beard that is thick, wiry, and coarse, with dull, rough hair, can counteract the interpretation of the chin. This belongs on the face of a moody, mean-spirited person, whose uncaring attitude and quick temper are easily provoked. If this type of beard grows close to the edges of the mouth, then the subject may suffer a violent serious injury in middle age.

## The Thin, Patchy Beard

If a beard is patchy or has thin, weak hairs, it suggests that the subject is weak and indecisive. It is similar in interpretation to the receding chin, but not quite as bad. The ancient Chinese considered this type of beard an indicator of ill health that gets worse as the subject ages. If there is a bald patch on the philtrum, the subject will be the subject of slander and criticism. Once again, this situation will worsen as age increases.

# About the Author

The late Jonathan Dee (1957–2010) was an outstanding astrologer, Tarot card reader, and psychic since the 1970s, having worked all over the UK and also in the USA. He was well known on radio, television, and in a variety of magazines as a serious historian and folklorist in addition to his other skills.

Until 2009, Dee was the regular daily astrologer for BBC Radio Wales for 23 years, on a program that is not only the most listened to in Wales, but which also received a Sony Award; all this besides broadcasting on many other radio stations and TV channels including BBC Radio 4, Talkradio UK, LBC, HTV, Granada, and Carlton, both as an astrologer and historian. He also presented a series of programs for BBC TV exploring the fascinating byways of the history of Wales.

A prolific author, Dee has written books on subjects as diverse as illustrated guides to Tarot, Runes, Feng Shui, Color Therapy, Chinese Face Reading, and Astrology as well as historical works on Ancient Egypt and the history of Prophecies.

Many of Jonathan Dee's books have been translated into foreign languages including Portuguese, Spanish, Finnish, Greek, and Japanese.

Jonathan Dee lived in Wales with his partner, Dean, until his untimely death in 2010; a great loss to all his friends, and an immense loss of an awesome fount of knowledge.